Hold You, Mommy

Hold You, Mommy

Laurie Lovejoy **Hilliard** | Sharon Lovejoy **Autry**

BETHANY HOUSE PUBLISHERS

Minneapolis Minnesota

Published by Bethany House Publishers
11400 Hampshire Avenue South
Bloomington, Minnesota 55438

Bethany House Publishers is a division of
Baker Publishing Group, Grand Rapids, Michigan.

Printed in the United States of America

ISBN-13: 978-0-7642-0198-1
ISBN-10: 0-7642-0198-0

Library of Congress Cataloging-in-Publication Data

Hilliard, Laurie Lovejoy.
 Hold you, Mommy : moments with God for moms on the go / Laurie Lovejoy Hilliard, Sharon Lovejoy Autry.
  p. cm.
 Summary: "This parenting devotional, written by the founders of 2MOMS women's ministry, is designed to give help and encouragement to mothers of young children. The 12-week study combines Scripture, personal remarks, activities, and suggested prayers. Includes a leader's guide with discussion questions for small group settings"—Provided by publisher.
  ISBN 0-7642-0198-0 (pbk.)
  1. Mothers—Religious life. 2. Mothers—Prayer books and devotions—English. 3. Mother and child—Religious aspects—Christianity. 4. Parenting—Religious aspects—Christianity. 5. Child rearing—Religious aspects—Christianity. I. Autry, Sharon Lovejoy. II. Title.

 BV4529.18.H55 2006
 242'.6431–dc22   2006007821

Dedication

This book is dedicated to our children:
Alec, Brittlea, Abby, Crislynn, Avery, Davis, and Addison.
Were it not for you, there would be no stories to tell.
We love you.

Acknowledgments

If you are a mom, you know how busy moms are, so we wanted you to know who helped us get this book to you. Thank you, thank you, thank you . . .

. . . To our husbands (Pat and Charles) and children, who encourage us to write but let us know how much they miss us when we are away.

. . . To Janie Henry for spending hours (and hours) reading and feeding us great ideas. You are a gentle critic, a faithful friend, and a remarkable prayer warrior for the Lord. We couldn't have done it without you!

. . . To Cynthia Harris for the great ideas for the book and a quiet place to write. You are such an encourager! We love you!

. . . To Dad and Mom for believing in the project even when we were a little unsure. Thank you for your endless prayers.

. . . To Megan Breedlove for allowing us to use her precious poem.

. . . To our editor, Jeanne Hedrick, for the deadline extensions and polishing the book. You are amazing!

. . . To those who prayed faithfully throughout this project and beyond.

. . . To our Board of Directors—thank you for your godly counsel, direction, and prayers.

. . . To our volunteers—you make ministry possible.

. . . To Joe and Dee Dee Clark for allowing us some precious quiet hours and a picturesque place to write.

. . . To moms across the country who shared their stories with us.

. . . And to the Lord, who has given us the privilege of being moms. For in that role we catch a glimpse of the amazing love He has for us. To Him we give all glory!

Table of Contents

Introduction

"HOLD YOU, MOMMY"... Such precious words spoken by children who have heard us say time and again, "Do you want Mommy to hold you?" As you read through this book, we pray that you will sense God's presence wrapping His arms around you. Just as you are tuned in to the needs of your children, the Lord wants to show you that He is just as attentive to you. He shows us how much He loves us by letting us love our children so deeply.

Several years ago, God inspired us to write a devotional book. This was to be a unique devotional because it would be divided into a different theme for each week (five days per week), and we would use the lyrics from the songs on our CD for moms, entitled *Hold You, Mommy* (*www.momandlovingit.org* for information). As you read, you'll find some of the words from the music scattered throughout the book. We hope that the words of the songs will meet you right where you are as they have for so many moms through the years.

We have also included a study guide at the end of the book for those of you meeting with other moms to discuss what you have read/learned. Each week does have a theme, so this makes it easier to get together with other moms to chat about what you have read and how it affected you. In addition to each day's reading, you will find a prayer (some written for you, others that you can write on your own) and a section called "Mama Drama." This segment is designed to help you "act out" (i.e., put into practice) what you have read that day. Use these ideas as you want, or don't use them if you haven't got the time that day. It is up to you.

So enjoy, Mom. We think you'll find that you aren't alone in your feelings and struggles. We are in this thing together. The Lord is on our side, and with Him, we always have hope. Thanks for picking up the book. May God "Hold You" and your family as you read.

Holding tightly to Him,
Sharon and Laurie

He's Always There

"Hold You, Mommy"

My heart is filled with joy as I hold you in my arms
Knowing all you want and all you need is truly found in me.
God's precious gift of love is all wrapped up in you.
I want to raise you up to love the Lord the way He wants me
    to.

I'll cherish each and every time I hold you in my arms.
Oh I know the days are passing much too fast.
But when this time has come and gone I'll hold the memory
Of your little arms extended up to me, saying. . . .

Hold you, Mommy. Hold you, Mommy.
Safe within your arms of love is where I long to be.
Hold you, Mommy. Oh hold you, Mommy
Just like the Father up above, surround me with Your perfect
    love again.

When you fall and skin your knee and come running back
    to me
I want to be the one to wipe your tears, kiss your hurts,
    calm your fears.
When you wake up in the night and cry out in the dark
I want to hold you close, whisper in your ear, "Everything
    will be alright."

I know there'll come a time when I won't hold you in
    my arms.
You won't need my hugs or want them anymore.
But how I want my arms to always be a refuge in your eyes
No matter where you roam or the changes in your life.

"Hold You, Mommy"

Handing her crying baby brother back to me, my eight-year-old daughter asked, "Why does Addison always stop crying when *you* hold him?"

"Well, honey," I explained, "He's been with me longer than you. Remember, he spent nine months in my tummy, so my voice is familiar and brings comfort to him. Somehow he feels safe when he is with me."

She seemed to understand, but I could tell by her furrowed brow that she didn't really like it. She longed to have the same power as "Mommy" had.

Children long to be with their parents. That's how God made us. When I worked in Child Protective Services several years ago, I found it interesting to watch children with their moms and dads. Even when they were in highly dysfunctional situations and could have been moved to a more secure and safe environment, children still preferred to be with their biological parent(s). As bad as their home was, it was all they had ever known, so they didn't want to leave it.

The phrase "Hold you, Mommy" may be familiar to you if you have a toddler in your home. I first heard these precious words when my firstborn, Alec, was beginning to talk. When he wanted me to hold him, he would hold his arms up and say, "Hold you, Mommy . . . hold you."

Some days, I'll admit, my most common response would be, "Just a minute, buddy." But when I really thought about his sweet little voice, my heart would melt! I had never heard a child say anything so cute!

Because I thought the phrase was so unique, I decided to write and record a song by that title. After singing it publicly for the first time at a mom's group, I instantly found out that my child was *not* the only child who had spoken the adorable words. Now, after singing it hundreds of times, I've discovered that it is actually a common saying among children.

As I ponder these sweet memories with my boys—Addison's

wanting to be with me, and Alec's charming words, "Hold you, Mommy"—I am keenly aware of my responsibility to my children. They depend on me. They desperately need me. They look to me to provide love, protection, and sustenance for their very lives.

Just as my children long to be near me, I realize my relationship with my heavenly Father is much the same. In John 10:4 (paraphrased) Jesus says that His sheep follow His voice because they recognize it. He would never force me, but He longs for me to come to Him and be near Him.

His strong arms are always waiting to lift me into His lap, if only I'll stop running long enough to reach up and call to Him. He desires for me to know *His* voice and not be distracted by the voices around me. He yearns for me to know the peace that He will provide when I abide in Him. He wants to offer comfort, protection, and sustenance for each day. He longs to hear me say, "Hold me, Lord."

If you haven't been climbing into His lap lately, start now. If you are His child, claim your position. John 1:12 says, "To all who received him, to those who believed in his name, he gave the right to become children of God." He's waiting with open arms to hold you. Rest in His arms today.

Lord, I am so busy being a mom that I don't always stop to be in your presence. I don't take the time to let you hold me. Forgive me, Lord, for thinking that I can provide what my children need without depending on your strength and wisdom. I commit this time to you, asking that you mold me and make me into the mom you want me to be. Hold me close. In Jesus name, amen.

MAMA**DRAMA**

When your children ask you to hold them today, stop and make time to do it. As you hold them, close your eyes and picture yourself with God's arms wrapped around you. Rest in Him.

When Avery was three years old, the last thing she would always ask me at bedtime was, "Mommy, will you hold me in the morning?" She was getting her request in early! Maybe you can let God "hold you" each morning as you work through this devotional guide.

Yes, Jesus Loves Me

HOW IS IT that adding a child to your family has a way of transforming your home? Children change our priorities. They change our sleep patterns. They change our finances. They change our relationships. They change pretty much everything! Mostly, however, they change our hearts. I had never experienced the depth of love I now know until I added children to my life.

Immediately after Avery was born, she was running a low-grade temperature. The doctors ordered IV antibiotics for her, just in case there was infection. After several attempts to start the IV, the nurses were unsuccessful. Her little veins were difficult to find.

A nurse came to our room to update us on the situation. She hesitantly explained, "Because we were unable to find a good vein in her arm or foot, we had to use the vein in her head." She assured us that it looked worse than it felt.

How does she *know?* I thought. *Has she ever had a needle poked in* her *head?* My heart was heavy. I was worried. And I was helpless. This was my baby, but I couldn't do anything to help her.

The following day the pediatrician came in and informed us that they wanted to do a test that would determine for sure whether Avery had an infection or not. When we asked how the test was performed, he began to describe how the nurse would roll Avery up in a ball until her little spine was protruding. The nurse would then hold her as still as possible while the doctor stuck a needle in her back at precisely the proper position in order to draw out some spinal fluid for the test.

I knew that I couldn't handle watching the procedure, so I asked if Charles, my husband, could be with her. They said, "No, we don't really think that is a good idea." In essence they were saying, "It is too difficult for a parent to watch." When they left the room I began to cry. I loved Avery more in just a few hours than I could have ever imagined. How could a child I'd never known be tugging at my heart so intensely?

The test was done. There was no infection. The IV was soon

removed, and we were able to go home the next day. What a relief for all of us!

The experience of raising children has given me a better understanding of how much God must love me. It's amazing to think that no matter how much I love my children, God's love for His children is even greater.

In Matthew 7:9–11 it says, "If you, then, though you are evil, know how to give good gifts to your children, how *much more* will your Father in heaven give good gifts to those who ask him!" (emphasis added). If we know how to give good things to our kids, just think how much better God is at loving *His* children.

God loves you and wants to reach out to you. Don't be afraid of Him. Think how much you love your children and then remember—He's much better at this than I could ever be! Take a look at Romans 8:31–39 from THE MESSAGE translation of the Bible. You can't deny how much God loves you when you read this.

> So, what do you think? With God on our side like this, how can we lose? If God didn't hesitate to put everything on the line for us, embracing our condition and exposing himself to the worst by sending his own Son, is there anything else he wouldn't gladly and freely do for us? And who would dare tangle with God by messing with one of God's chosen? Who would dare even to point a finger? The One who died for us — who was raised to life for us!—is in the presence of God at this very moment sticking up for us. Do you think anyone is going to be able to drive a wedge between us and Christ's love for us? There is no way! Not trouble, not hard times, not hatred, not hunger, not homelessness, not bullying threats, not backstabbing, not even the worst sins listed in Scripture . . . None of this fazes us because Jesus loves us. I'm absolutely convinced that nothing—nothing living or dead, angelic or demonic, today or tomorrow, high or low, thinkable or unthinkable—absolutely *nothing* can get between us and God's love because of the way that Jesus our Master has embraced us (emphasis added).

So do you get it? . . . *God loves you!* Thank Him and live like a loved child today because . . . you are!

Lord Jesus, thank you for your love. It is hard for me to accept that you love me so much when I feel so undeserving. As I love my children, continue to open my eyes to see how much you love me. I want to rest in your love. I don't have to try to prove myself to you. You did all the work on the cross, so that all I have to do is focus on you! In your name I pray, amen.

MAMA**DRAMA**

When you're feelin' kinda low, remember . . . with God on your side, how can you lose? A friend of ours shared that when she's down, her daughter sings to her . . .

> Jesus loves all the mommies,
> All the mommies of the world,
> Red, brown, yellow, black, and white
> They are precious in His sight,
> Jesus loves all the mommies of the world.

Sleepless in the Battle

I DON'T THINK my back has ever hurt as badly as it did last week. You know that terrible ache right between your shoulder blades, that sharp pain that shoots up your neck and back down again? You know that "standing with a baby in your arms too long" pain? I was just sure that even my chiropractor wouldn't be able to straighten me out again! My pain was triggered by several nights of walking the floor with a sick four-month-old baby who weighs a whopping seventeen pounds.

Viral croup has run rampant in our household over the past two weeks, taking casualties as it went. My five-year-old was hit first. She was miserable for six long days. I was determined that I would do all I could to keep the bug from attacking any more of my troops.

We had a strict hand-washing regimen; I quarantined the sick child (as much as you can in the same house) and opened the windows. But even with my best efforts, the baby started "barking" just as the first child began to recover. I was overwhelmed and exhausted. I was *so* ready to be done with this.

I thought my nights were sleepless before the baby got sick. They were actually a breeze; I just didn't know it. One night I was up with him at least *ten times*. Each time he awakened, I got up and whisked him off to the bathroom where the steam from the shower would finally calm him and ease his breathing. I would then hold and bounce him until he finally fell asleep again.

Then I would, very carefully, maneuver myself onto the bed in an elevated lying position, hoping to sneak a little nap before the cycle began again. It was a long night. Can you feel my pain?

I was pooped the next day and simply dreaded the thought of another night like the last. I just kept thinking, "God, I want to be there for my baby when he is sick, but I'm so tired. I don't think I can make it another night without sleep."

Sleep, what a wonderful commodity—if only I could have some! Thankfully, my husband took a shift the next night and allowed me to sleep for three solid hours. It was just enough to get me through the following night. (Which was good because that was the night my husband got sick!)

It was several nights before normal sleep returned to our home. As I reflected on this whole "sleepless in the battle" scene, I realized *my* ability to care for my children is *limited.* As badly as I want to always be there to meet the needs of my children, I am physically limited in what I can do. I can become sleep deprived and emotionally exhausted. I don't always know exactly what to do for my children. I am busy and not always available for them. And as they grow older, I won't always be around when they need me.

I'm so thankful that God's ability to care for me is *not* limited. God does not need sleep. God is always there. "My help comes from the Lord, the Maker of heaven and earth. He who watches over you will not slumber. . . . the Lord will watch over your coming and going both now and forevermore" (Psalm 121:2–3, 8).

For some of you it is difficult to believe that God is always going to be there for you. You cannot imagine a father who never sleeps or tires of hearing from you. Maybe your parents were not there for you, either physically or emotionally. You never felt you could go to them with your needs.

But remember: God, the heavenly Father, is not like your earthly parents. He's *never* too tired and He never walks away. He is *always available.* As you face your daily battles, He's saying, "'Never will I leave you; never will I forsake you.' So we say with confidence, 'The Lord is my helper; I will not be afraid'" (Hebrews 13:5–6). Trust Him.

Dear Sleepless One, thank you for assuring me that you will always be with me. I am so glad that I never have to worry about your walking out on me when times get tough. Thank you that you will never tire of my coming to you either, even for the same mistakes and struggles. I praise you, Father, for being there when I need you—even if it is in the middle of the night. You never sleep. You never slumber. Thank you that I can be confident, knowing that when I'm in desperate need of you, you are "Sleepless in the Battle." I love you. Amen.

MAMA**DRAMA**

The next time you have a sick child and are not getting as much sleep as you need, remember: Your God never sleeps and is always ready to meet your needs.

Instead of dreading the time when your children are sick, use the time to create a special "snuggle time." Maybe rent some movies, color together, or just sit and hold each other. Your kids will remember your being there when they needed it most.

The Hairs on Your Head Are Numbered

I LIKE DETAILS, don't you? Paying attention to the details is usually a good thing, right? Many times, after my husband hangs up the phone, I'll begin questioning him about his conversation. His usual reply to my question is, "I don't know . . . I didn't ask."

Didn't ask! I'll think. *How can you carry on a conversation and not find out the important details?* To my amazement, he has neglected to gather the information that I deem necessary, pertinent, and vital to the conversation. Now, if I had asked him the score of an important football game five years ago, he could probably provide me with more details than I care to know! Aren't men funny? The details that matter so much to us usually don't matter very much to them.

There is no one, however, who pays greater attention to details than our Creator. God is the ultimate "detail person." Just look at the perfectly formed flowers, clothed in vibrant colors. Consider the majestic trees waving gracefully in the wind, and the vast starry sky on a clear night. Think about the brightly colored bugs in all their different shapes and sizes. God is absolutely amazing!

His creation declares His attention to details. In all His creation, however, nothing compares to the detail involved in the creation of human life. Talk about details! How long has it been since you studied human anatomy? Our bodies are truly remarkable, aren't they?

While nursing my four-month-old baby, I was made aware of God's careful attention to details. I began to notice all the wonderful little features that made my baby unique—his tiny, chubby fingers curled around mine, his perfect rosy lips pressed against my breast, his soft velvety head sprouting new hair, his squishy little legs, creased as if sectioned off by rubber bands, and his small fat toes resembling miniature peanuts. What an incredibly detailed creation!

As moms, we shuffle a tremendous number of details in our

lives, don't we? Feeding schedules, laundry, doctor appointments, play dates, family meal planning, running errands, getting kids to their practices and games, etc. The list could go on and on.

I don't know about you, but I can easily get bogged down in all the details of my life. I grow overwhelmed as I try to stay in *control* of it all. I sometimes feel guilty asking God for strength or help in the midst of the chaos. After all, I created it, so I must handle it! Right?

Wrong. We shouldn't ever hesitate to invite God in on the details of our days. He already knows them, and He cares enough to want to be a part of them. In Luke 12:6–7 it says, "Are not five sparrows sold for two pennies? Yet not one of them is forgotten by God. Indeed, the very hairs of your head are all numbered. Don't be afraid; you are worth more than many sparrows."

Why would God have mentioned that He knows the number of hairs on our heads if He didn't care about the details of our lives? Don't be afraid; come to Him with the details. You are worth more than any old sparrow! Include Him in the smallest details of your life, even those that may seem insignificant to you. Remember, He cares about *the number of hairs* on your head. You can't get much smaller than that!

> *Creator in heaven, how majestic is your name in all the earth. Nature shouts of your attention to detail. I praise you and thank you! I am in awe of you as I gaze at the works of your hands. I am humbled, Lord, to think that you care more about me than any other created thing. Thank you for caring about the details of my life, no matter how small or seemingly insignificant they may be. I need your wisdom and direction today. I want the details of my life to line up with your plans and purposes for me. For it is your plans (details) that will prevail (Proverbs 19:21). Thank you, Father, that I can come to you just as I am . . . through Jesus. Amen.*

MAMA**DRAMA**

Go into your child's room after he or she goes to sleep. Look at the details in his or her face. Thank God for caring about the details in our lives.

Take time to stop and really examine a flower or plant. Look at the wonderful detail involved. Thank God for caring about the details in your life today, and invite Him to rule over every one.

Heavenly Hide-and-Seek

SHE WAS TIRED of shopping, but I wasn't quite finished. (Isn't that how it usually is with our children . . . and husbands?) There were only a couple of other people in our area of the store, so when she asked if she could play hide-and-seek, I gave her safe boundaries and away she went.

A few moments later I started looking for her, shoving the clothes with both hands to check the middle of the racks (every kid's perfect hiding place), looking behind the jeans along the wall, through the racks again, and then suddenly I was frantic.

Thinking she must have disobeyed, I started looking outside of the boundaries—under the doors of the dressing rooms and behind the checkout counter. I gave a stern, "Come out right now," and out popped her head from a rack clearly within the boundaries. I breathed a sigh of relief, and greeted her with open arms.

In Luke 15:4 Jesus said, "Suppose one of you has a hundred sheep and loses one of them. Does he not leave the ninety-nine . . . and go after the lost sheep until he finds it?" I was determined that day to find my "lost sheep." My concern at the moment was not that she had gone out of the boundaries, but that I *find her.*

Just as we would look for our children, Jesus also continues "seeking" us until we are found. We would never say, "Oh, I have *most* of my children. That's fine. We can go on without that one." Jesus doesn't want to leave any child behind either. He isn't concerned that we have crossed the boundary lines or done things that we shouldn't have done. His concern is that we are found.

Just as we don't stop loving our children because they aren't perfect, God doesn't stop loving us because we've done things wrong. Some people think they have to get their life totally together before they can say yes to God. But that's getting things backward. He wants to guide us so our lives can be all He created us to be.

Have you been found? Or are you still hiding? Is it time for you to come out of the shadows? Maybe it's not that you're hiding from Him; you're just lost and you know something is missing in your life. Let Him find you. He is ready to receive you. He's waiting with arms open wide, a sigh of relief, and a big smile on His face.

MAMA**DRAMA**

We haven't forgotten the prayer. We are going to let you write your own prayer after you've had time to think on the following things.

If you have never asked Jesus to come into your heart, would you like to be "found" today? You can use the lines below to write a prayer, asking Him to: (1) forgive your sins (all those times you've stepped out of the boundaries), and (2) come into your life. If you have more questions, there are Bible verses listed at the end of the book (Who Am I?) that can help you find some answers.

If you have already accepted Christ, feel free to review the verses in there and thank Him for His grace and mercy toward you. You can use the lines below to write a prayer of thanks to Him.

If you are in doubt about your relationship with Jesus—"Have I really been found?"—you need to read John 10:28 and Romans 8:38–39. They confirm that when He comes into your heart, He stays, and once you're found you're never lost out of His hand again.

_____

_____

_____

_____

_____

_____

_____

Comfort in the Chaos

"So we're not giving up. How could we!
Even though on the outside it often looks
like things are falling apart on us, on the
inside, where God is making new life, not
a day goes by without His unfolding grace.
These hard times are small potatoes compared to the coming good times, the lavish
celebration prepared for us. There's far
more here than meets the eye. The things
we see now are here today, gone tomorrow.
But the things we can't see now will last
forever."

2 Corinthians 4:16–18 (THE MESSAGE)

You Are Not Alone

As MANY OF YOU know, I have entered the world of diapers, strollers, and middle-of-the-night feedings again. Most of the time "I'm loving it," but other times I think "I'm losing it!" I don't know about you, but I find myself forgetting things (primarily my children's names), or I'll go to another room to get something and forget why I'm there. Sometimes thinking of a simple word can bumfuzzle me! And have you ever put something away and then for the life of you, you can't remember where you put it? Please tell me you can relate . . . or am I just getting old? I prefer to think that it is postpartum brain loss.

Feeling "confused and disoriented" is a problem for most moms. A common occurrence in our house that can almost bring me to tears is when everyone needs me at the same time. The baby awakens from his nap, crying because he's hungry, and my five-year-old is in the bathroom calling, "Mommy, I neeeeeeed you!" My eight-year-old, standing on her head, determined to keep her balance, is breathlessly saying, "Mommy, Mommy, look at me, look at me!" And at the exact same time, my ten-year-old is asking, "Mom, can I buy these new bracelets off eBay? The deal goes off in five minutes."

Of course all this is happening as I'm preparing dinner. And while working quickly to put out the various family "fires," I find I've started one of my own on the stove! I've often had the thought, *If one more person calls my name, I'm gonna scream,* only to hear my husband say, "Honey, have you seen my glasses?" Aahh! I can't take it anymore!

There are days I think, *Lord, I* can't *do this. I don't even have the energy to try anymore.* Some days the challenges of motherhood are too demanding, too overwhelming, too exhausting.

Do you ever feel like giving up? Is your burden too heavy? Are you afraid because you feel out of control? Don't worry—you are not alone.

Isaiah 41:10 says, "So do not *fear*, for I am with you; do not be *dismayed*, for I am your God. *I* will *strengthen* you and help you; *I* will *uphold* you with my righteous right hand" (emphasis added). It isn't all up to you. God longs to fill us with His strength if we'll just let Him. It is in recognizing our *weakness* that we realize God's *strength*. Isaiah 40:29 says it well: "He gives strength to the weary and increases the power of the weak."

In *The Message*, Isaiah 41:9–10 reads like this: "I've picked you. I haven't dropped you. Don't panic. I'm with you. There's no need to fear for I'm your God. I'll give you strength. I'll help you. I'll hold you steady, keep a firm grip on you."

Just remember: When *you* are *out of control, He* is *in control.* Get close to Him. Seek Him, and He'll empower you to handle the challenges that overwhelm you.

Lord, I want to stop trying to do everything on my own. I need you to calm my spirit, to give me strength, to hold me steady. Give me self-control so that I can respond gently instead of harshly, set loving limits instead of rash rules, and seek to understand before making demands. Lord, I am weak, but you are strong! Thanks be unto God! Amen.

MAMA**DRAMA**

The next time everyone wants you at the same time, yell, "Time out!" Play a fun game by lining them up so you can take their requests one at a time.

Another way to make the situation less tense is to ask the kids, "Is there anyone else who could have helped you besides Mom?" If they have siblings encourage them to help each other.

The Terrible, Horrible, No Good, Very Bad Day

*I*T WAS A TERRIBLE, horrible, no good, very bad day. Things were not going as planned! I had been busy all morning but had nothing to show for it. I had intended to get up early, but instead I slept late. I had been ugly to my kids. It was afternoon, and I hadn't even had time to take a shower. I was feeling really low, primarily about myself. I was in a funk.

Alec, my ten-year-old, hugged me that day and out of the blue said, "I'm so glad you're my mom. I wouldn't want anyone else." I returned the hug and commented, "Sometimes I think someone else could do a much better job." He looked at me with a horrified look and said, "Why would you say that?"

Why *would* I say something like that? I guess because I felt like a complete failure. I was not being patient with my kids. I had raised my voice one too many times. A harsh scowl seemed to be permanently chiseled into my face. I was comparing myself with other moms. *I don't deserve to have kids,* I thought.

Guilt weighs heavily on most of our shoulders at one time or another. It seems to go with the title of Mother. No one prepared us for how challenging this role would be. Nor did they tell us how connected our hearts would be to our children.

I received an email from a mom who was feeling rotten about herself. She wrote, "My six-year-old son took the time to sound out and write on his chalkboard, *I HATE MOM*. I am a little destroyed and feel very hurt," she shared.

Our children can cause us to rise to the heights of parental bliss or, in a fleeting moment, slump to the depths of parental misery. It is difficult to separate our image of *who* we really are from who we *think* we should be. We are trying to live up to some unwritten code of perfect "mom-dom." Of course, no one knows what the code really says. We just know we are not living up to it.

I heard a friend say one time, "God wants me to be a 'good' mom, not a perfect one." But sadly many of us are striving for perfection. What we don't realize is that these ideals we have ascribed to ourselves are impossible to keep, and they only make everyone (the people around us as well as ourselves) miserable. Nobody likes to be around people who think they are perfect or won't admit they're wrong. So why put ourselves through all that?

I want to encourage you today. The next time you're having a terrible, horrible, no good, very bad day, remember: The only "code" we are to be patterning our life after is God's Word. We are to base our self-image on who He says we are. Ephesians 2:10 says it well: "For we are God's workmanship, created in Christ Jesus to do good works, which God prepared in advance for us to do."

Don't fall into the trap of self-defeat. Let God untangle the web of lies you've believed about yourself and set you free to find *who you are in Him*—a daughter of the King, worthy because of His shed blood, forgiven by His grace, and strengthened by His strong hand.

> *Lord Jesus, I feel like such a failure at times. I don't feel I even deserve to be a mom because of how I've acted toward my family lately. Please forgive me, Lord, and restore me to a right relationship with you. Help me find myself in you. Help me sift through the lies I've believed for so long, and replace them with your truth of who I really am. Thank you for covering me with your righteousness, so that I am not continually trying to be good enough on my own. In your strength I'll seek to focus on you and not me! Amen.*

MAMA**DRAMA**

When your children give you an unexpected compliment (like "I'm so glad that you're my mom"), write it down in a notebook. On discouraging days it will cheer you up to look back and remember how their love made you feel.

Singing can be a great tool for breaking out of a funk. If you can commit to memory some songs based on God's Word and your position in Him, they will come in handy on terrible, horrible, no good, very bad days.

The Truth Helps

MY LAST SEMESTER of college was a flurry of life-changing activities. I was planning my December wedding, my then-fiancé and I were building our first house, and I was trying to student teach. In the midst of all of this, my dad had to be rushed to the hospital in the middle of the night because we thought he was having a heart attack. (He wasn't. Praise God!)

I arrived at school that day with my mind at the hospital, exhausted and worried. I stood before the class, trying to teach the students something about tomatoes. (How interesting that it had to be to a bunch of eight-year-olds.) The attention span of one little guy was gone and he made some comment, probably like, "I don't even like tomatoes. Why do we have to learn about 'em?"

The dam broke. I dropped my head and started bawling, right in front of the class. Those poor kids didn't know what to do. They sat there with their mouths open, chins in their hands, and eyes glued to me. I heard them scolding the child who became "the straw that broke the camel's back."

Finally I gained enough control to let them in on what had been happening in my life. With that honesty, suddenly I wasn't just a teacher; I was a person who had feelings—somebody who needed them. One by one, they came and gave me hugs. Then the rest of the week they were (mostly) great. When somebody would act out, the other kids took care of it on their own, saying, "Stop it! You'll make Miss Lovejoy cry again!" or "You're not being very nice! She's havin' a hard time!"

Do you have a hard time letting your family in on your feelings? I do. But I've found that when the game face is gone, and I offer my children a real person with joys and hurts, they are much more understanding. It helps when I say things like, "Mommy is just having a hard time being happy today. Mommy is sad because my friend is sick," or "Mommy has said yes to lots of things so now I'm feeling too busy."

Letting my favorite people in the world into my struggles not only gives them the opportunity to minister to me, but it also takes the pressure off by lightening the burden a little. The Bible says, "When you're in over your head, I'll be there with you. When you're in rough waters, you will not go down. When you're between a rock and a hard place, it won't be a dead end—Because I am God, your personal God" (Isaiah 43:2–3a THE MESSAGE).

Sometimes God uses my family to keep me from going under. When I share with my kids and husband, it helps them know I'm not necessarily angry with them. It's just me, the circumstances, or my body. My sister-in-law told her girls that once a month she would be in a funk. Instead of trying to hide it, she was honest with them. Now they ask her, "Mom, is today that day that you have a hard time being happy?" What's bad is when you're just "in a mood" and there's no excuse!

Laurie explained it to her kids this way: "When you grow up, you have these things called hormones that make you feel ways you don't want to feel." Her daughter said, "Do all mommies have that?" "Yes," Laurie told her. Then she asked, "Will I have those when I'm a mommy?"

Oh, the glory days of childhood! Several weeks later, her son was having a bad day. When she asked him what was wrong he said, "I think I'm gettin' my hormones."

Are you having one of those days when you feel like you're in over your head? If so, let your family share your struggles, and pour out all your feelings to the Lord. He promises that He is with you, no matter what you are going through. Tell the truth. It does help.

Lord, _____

_____

_____

_____

Because of Jesus, amen.

MAMA**DRAMA**

The next time your spirits are low because of circumstances, exhaustion, or that monthly visitor, let your family know why you're struggling. They can help to lighten your load.

Don't Look Too Closely,
part one

AS MOMS, we have a tendency to focus on what is right in front of us. Rest is hard to find in the midst of it all. I once read of a servant who told how his master found rest.

> Occasionally (he) would arrange his morning so as to be free for a little while shortly before noon. Then he would ask me to accompany him to one of the upper floors of the palace, from a window of which he could look out into the far distance.
>
> "Space is medicine for eyes that have always to look at things too closely," he told me. "Those far mountains rest me." [1]

As moms, we become accustomed to "looking at things too closely." We see the clothes wadded and wrinkled on the floor, the sibling conflict that seems to go on and on, the flowers we would like to plant, the never ending loads of laundry, the projects started, the beds to make, and the meals to prepare. We analyze everything our husband says, and we wonder what our friend meant by her quick phone call. In that kind of environment, like standing in the middle of a city filled with buildings, it's hard to see clearly.

In all of that confusion we miss the "mountains" that could rest us. The Creator of the mountains longs to be our strength in the midst of the chaos. Jesus said, "I have come into the world as a light, so that no one who believes in me should stay in darkness" (John 12:46). He can shine light on our circumstances when we spend time with Him each day.

Let Him know you're struggling. Talk with Him as you feel your blood pressure rising after seeing your child is still shoeless when you've already told her seventeen times to put them on. Maybe you don't see mountains every day, but you do see what God created: trees, flowers, snow, the sunshine, and, most important, our children and husbands. Thanking Him for those things can give you rest from the daily grind of life.

Are you in need of rest? Do you need medicine for your eyes that have been "looking at things too closely" lately, analyzing every aspect of your life or trying to keep up with the demands? I love the song "Turn Your Eyes Upon Jesus." It reminds me to look to Him in the chaos. He is the rest that we need.

> "Turn your eyes upon Jesus
> Look full in His wonderful face
> And the things of earth will grow strangely dim
> In the light of His glory and grace." [2]

How do we in the midst of our chaos turn our eyes upon Him? Tomorrow we will explore that in a deeper way. "I look up to the mountains; does my strength come from mountains? No, my strength comes from God, who made heaven, and earth, and mountains" (Psalm 121:1–2 THE MESSAGE).

> *Lord, you know how I see my family. You alone know the struggles that I face and the joys I celebrate. You know what would rest me. Help me to turn my eyes to you when life is chaotic, and help me to seek rest from you. Thank you for knowing the big picture when all I can see is what is going on inside the walls of my house. As I see the things you have created, including my family, may it cause me to look up with a grateful heart. Let your creation be a reminder to turn my eyes upon you. In Jesus' name I pray, amen.*

MAMA**DRAMA**

What is it that rests you? Sit for a moment (even if it is a loud moment) and let your mind wander to the mountains, a stream, your grandmother's cookies, or the faces of your children. Take a mini vacation! Thank God for those images and for His ability to give us rest even in the chaos.

Don't Look Too Closely, part two

*I*N THE AFTERNOON, before it's time to make dinner, the kids are restless. I usually haven't accomplished as much as I'd hoped, and the house is a wreck from living life too quickly. My husband comes home from work and, rather than being glad to see him, I'm a harried mess! It's at that moment that I need a room on an upper floor with a window and a view of the mountains to rest me! Wouldn't that be nice?

"If I keep my eyes on God, I won't trip over my own feet" (Psalm 25:15 THE MESSAGE).

With all the demands of mothering, how do we keep from tripping—if not on our own feet, then on the tent that our five-year-old constructed in the living room or the piles of clothes someone left on the floor? How do we keep our eyes on God so that we aren't seeing life too closely, missing many of the blessings in our days?

Jesus said, "I am the bread that gives life. Whoever comes to me will never be hungry" (John 6:35 NCV). Just as our physical bodies need food and water every day, our spirits need the life that comes from Jesus. I don't know about you, but I need food for my soul more now, as a mom, than ever before. I've sometimes found myself in spiritual starvation mode when I make a habit of staying up too late watching TV, cleaning the house, or tending a baby or sick toddler to the point of exhaustion.

When I don't take time to be with the Lord, I find myself in a drought—a spiritual drought. Looking back, I can see my downward spiral during those days as I constantly compared myself to others, spoke nothing but discouragement to my husband, and had zero patience with my children for even the smallest thing they did that irritated me.

Even though *I know* the benefits of turning my eyes to the Lord, of feasting on the bread of life that He offers every day, and experiencing the patience and strength that He offers, it still doesn't come naturally. It takes an intentional effort.

I remember nursing my children during the early morning hours. I was in and out of sleep, but I had my Bible next to my comfy chair, and I took the time to read short passages from it each day. Now that my kids are older, it takes setting an alarm clock to jostle me out of my sleep so I can tiptoe to my quiet spot. I've found that time spent with the Lord is never wasted, even if I don't feel better immediately.

We can always find some time that works to spend time with God. It can be in the morning before the kids rise, during the day when they are otherwise occupied, or after they go to bed. Whenever you find the time that works for you, begin by asking Him to open your spiritual eyes so you can see what He has for you.

Don't be content to just read His Word. Study and memorize it, and discuss it with other believers when you have the chance. Pick one word from a passage to really focus on and let it enrich your understanding (*www.studylight.org* is a great help with a study like this).

From time to time, hire a babysitter and head to a coffee shop with your Bible and a journal for some quality study time. You could even consider checking into a hotel for a night to give you some quality time with God. Share openly with Him your joys, struggles, and disappointments as they happen, and linger in His presence until you receive the peace you are seeking.

During those overwhelming and frustrating days, make time for Him—no matter how brief the time may be. When you actively take steps to turn your eyes upon Jesus, you will find it makes all the difference. He gives comfort in the chaos.

> *Lord, it is easy for me to look at every detail of my life and drown in my circumstances. Forgive me for trying to handle all of it on my own when you are so willing to help. Please forgive me for being too busy to spend time with you. I need the life that you give when I devote time to our relationship. Grow me, Lord. Teach me. Go with me today. Turning my eyes to you, I pray in Jesus' name. Amen.*

MAMA**DRAMA**

Take a shower with purpose! Use that time to turn your heart to the Lord. Pray about your moment-by-moment concerns, or just be quiet and listen for Him to speak.

Here are some ideas for turning your eyes upon Him on the go:

1. Write Scripture verses on the mirror with dry-erase markers.

2. Play a CD of Scripture songs, like *Hide 'em in Your Heart* (Steve Green) or one of the *Seeds* Scripture collections (*Seeds of Faith; Seeds of Courage*, etc.)[3]

Getting to Know God

"Those who know the Lord
trust him,
because he will not leave those
who come to him."

Psalm 9:10 (NCV)

If I Could Only Remember

RECENTLY, I HAD the same conversation with two different ladies. They both told me that they hadn't been spending time with God, but when they do, they really are better wives and moms. One mom said, "After I spend time with Him, I get better. Then I forget God again."

I was right there with them, wondering why I too could spend time with the Lord, see the benefits, then forget to devote time to Him. I once heard Bible teacher Beth Moore say, "God delights when hearts, so prone to wander, choose Him."

It's a common thing for humans, especially moms, to try to handle everything on our own. Besides, there is so much to do that we think we don't have time for one more thing. The ironic thing is, though, when I stop and spend time with God, *I accomplish so much more.* It's like guaranteed help, and who of us doesn't need help?

Yet there are those times when I still forget to spend time with God. There are many things that can make our hearts wander, demands that consume our time. I found this entry in my journal and thought it might entice us all to turn our eyes back to Him. It can remind us of His faithfulness and help us remember the blessings that come when we give Him part of our hectic and chaotic days.

December 2004

About a week ago, I was low . . . very low. At a time that I felt I couldn't do anything right, I did do two things right: I started praying (those SOS prayers—"Please help fast, Lord!") and I began spending time with God, reading my Bible. I didn't feel better immediately, but I'm realizing the important thing is to know I *will* feel better. God has been so gracious to show me that over and over again. When I'm feeling down, if that low time draws me closer to Him—great! He is faithful to hold on to me and remind me of my purpose when I feel worthless. When I haven't been faithful in spending time with Him, He remains consistently loyal—always ready to take my hand and help me up. But I have to offer my hand and stop trying to get out of the quicksand of life and the mud of emotions on my own. He is my rescuer.

Are you trying to handle everything on your own? If you have never accepted Christ, asking Him to come into your life gives you someone to walk with each day, and it gives you hope when you're feeling down. No matter what you've done, He loves you. He really, *really* loves you!

If you are a believer, how long has it been since you made time for the Lord in your day? Don't miss out on the blessings that await your willingness to turn your wandering, busy, sleep-deprived heart toward Him for even a few minutes today. Choose Him and then trust Him to rescue you when you find yourself downhearted. If it's been a while since you talked with Him, pray—even if you have to pray an SOS prayer. He loves hearing from you.

December 2004 (continued)

Thank you, Lord, for being so different from my "get what you deserve" mentality. It's hard for me to see past that thought to the truth of who you are: Love—simply love. Just because you want to love me, you love me. Thank you, thank you, thank you for calling me back to you again and again. I love you, too! Living and learning in Jesus' name . . . Amen.

MAMA**DRAMA**

If you are a nursing mom, have your Bible handy and read one of the Psalms while you nurse. Before you begin reading, ask God to open your heart so you can see what He wants you to see.

Put your Bible in the car and sneak times with God as you wait for the kids to get out of school, wait your turn in the drive-thru, and sit in your car while your kids are napping in their car seats.

Praise the Lord

ONE NIGHT before we had a speaking engagement, I had a lot on my mind. I was in no shape to speak to women about loving their families, because at the moment I didn't think too much of mine. Mostly my husband. I was so mad at him! I felt like we (the kids and I) were an afterthought in his life.

I was fuming as I left our bus and headed for the church. Suddenly I saw the sunset. It was beautiful. I had almost missed it in my fury. I started walking slower and thanked God for the sunset. Then I saw the flag flying outside the church, and I thanked God for our country and the freedom to worship as we want.

It began a waterfall of thanks in my heart. I thanked Him for my family—for my children who were so precious and my husband, who was just having a bad day. I thanked God for loving me, for having the ability to stop me in my pious condemnation and turn my eyes to Him.

By the time I made my way to the door of the church, I didn't want to go in because my time of praise to the Lord was so sweet. My heart, which had just moments earlier been so heavy, was now full of love, forgiveness, and gratefulness. I was amazed at the instant change that praising the Lord had made in my heart and attitude.

When we praise the Lord, it isn't just a way for us to worship Him, although that is very important. "Praise releases the power of God into our lives. Praise is a powerful tool that the Lord has put in our hands to turn the difficult situations of our lives around." [1]

I realized that praise doesn't necessarily change our circumstances, but it can change our perspective and attitude about our situations. It gives hope for the challenging times. As days passed, I began acknowledging the amazing things about God as I prayed, instead of only making requests and asking forgiveness for things I had done wrong.

Praise doesn't come naturally for me. Before I ask anything from the Lord, I speak some words of praise to Him. It's not always easy, but practicing helps. "Let praise cascade off my lips; after all, you've taught me the truth about life! Invigorate my soul so I can praise you well" (Psalm 119:171, 175 THE MESSAGE).

Lord, I praise you for giving us the ability to praise you. You are the king of all the earth. Nothing is above you. You are the beginning, the end, and everything in between. Thank you for your creation. The trees, mountains, flowers, rivers, and especially people are all amazing gifts from you. I pray that you will let praise cascade off my lips, specific praises every day, all the time.

I ask that you help me learn to see the good things about my family, the blessings rather than the burdens. Would you remind me to daily praise you for them? Thank you. On my own, change is hopeless, but with you, my whole heart can be renewed. My attitude can change from sour to sweet. Thank you for loving me enough to die for me. Thank you for never giving up on me. Thank you for enabling us to be thankful. Thank you that we aren't condemned to just be negative; there is hope for tomorrow. Let everything that is within me praise you, Lord, and through that praise fill me with your strength and hope, letting that joy spill over into my family. I love you, Lord. I pray in Jesus' name, amen.

MAMADRAMA

Praise the Lord . . .

Thank Him aloud or in your head for everything: the sun that is so dependable, our country, your children, your home, your car, your life. Sing your words of praise to Him if you want.

The book of Psalms is in the middle of the Bible. It is a great place to read the praises of others written to the Lord. Some of our favorite psalms are: Psalm 34, 37, 40, 51, 84, 91, 103, 127, 139, and 145.

Waiting

*D*O YOU HAVE trouble waiting? I do. I find myself always looking for the shortest route to my destination, the shortest
checkout line at the grocery store, and the shortest cooking time
for the meal I'm making. I can be a very impatient person. I don't
particularly like sitting at long red lights. I am frustrated by the
time it takes to rewind a VHS tape. I am amazed that anyone can
use anything but high-speed Internet to get anything done. I'm
irritated at the time it takes my children to *find* their shoes, and
I'm sometimes annoyed by how long it takes them to *tie* the shoes
after they've found them.

We are products of our society. We have microwaves that cook
food quickly. We have cell phones that connect us immediately.
We have instant messaging, which sends our messages without
delay. We have digital cameras, which allow us to view pictures
we have taken instantaneously. We have shipping companies that
guarantee next-day delivery. Success is measured in how much
you can get done faster. We don't like waiting, and in most situations, we don't have to do much of it.

However, there are a few problems I see with the way in which
we are living. Besides this lifestyle resulting in sometimes intoler-
ant, self-centered, and stressed-out individuals, it goes against the
very nature of God. He doesn't get in a hurry.

I've heard it said, "God is rarely early, never late, and always
on time." He doesn't live according to our fast-paced society.
Maybe that is why we are not getting to know Him—we don't feel
we have the time, and we don't know how to slow our hearts down
to hear Him.

As I looked up Scriptures containing the word *wait* or *waiting*,
I discovered that most of them tied *waiting* to some response
from God. Only in waiting can we hear from God. I was convicted.
Here are a few verses that talk about waiting on God. Before you
read them, ask God to speak to your heart through them.

> Psalm 27:14: "Wait for the Lord; be strong and take heart
> and wait for the Lord."

Psalm 40:1: "I waited patiently for the Lord; he turned to me and heard my cry."

Psalm 130:5: "I wait for the Lord, my soul waits, and in his word I put my hope."

Isaiah 30:18: "Yet the Lord longs to be gracious to you; he rises to show you compassion. For the Lord is a God of justice. Blessed are all who wait for him!"

Romans 8:25: "But if we hope for what we do not yet have, we wait for it patiently."

Psalm 37:7: "Be still before the Lord and wait patiently for him; do not fret when men succeed in their ways, when they carry out their wicked schemes."

Are you in a time of waiting? You can be assured that while you are waiting on God, your time will not be wasted. Trust Him. Remember, He is always on time.

Lord, help me be still in your presence right now. My mind is cluttered with all the things that must be accomplished today, but for this moment I want to sit at your feet and wait on you as I meditate on your Word. Speak to my heart, O God. Fill me up, Lord. Give me the willingness and perseverance to wait on you. Amen.

MAMADRAMA

Try sitting still for one minute. Don't pray or talk to anyone else. Before you start, however, ask God to speak to you. Then just wait. Make a habit of doing this each day, even if it is just for a moment. Sometimes I'm like my friend's little girl who said, "I asked God a question, but I can't hear Him answer because my mind keeps talking." How true that is . . . wait on the Lord today!

Loud Times With God

*C*ARLY IN MY mothering career I shared a frustration with a friend who had older children. I was feeling defeated because I was having a hard time spending time with God. I was tired. I didn't know how I could wake up any earlier. When I did wake up early, it seemed like the baby could smell me and would wake up just minutes after my feet hit the floor. I felt sure that God was angry with me and ready to go look somewhere else for a faithful mom.

My friend told me, "Sharon, God knows your heart and He is very aware of the seasons of our lives. He isn't sitting up there shaking His finger at you. He's right beside you as you change diapers. When you're up in the night, so is He."

She went on to tell me that when her kids were small, she had felt the same way; she kept waiting for a "quiet time" to spend with God. One day the Lord revealed to her that she could spend time with Him even if it was a *loud time*. So with her son playing around her feet, she sat down and had a loud time with God.

God never said, "Spend quiet time with me every day in the morning, or else!" He encourages us to spend the time, to be still and know that He is God. He knows that hiding His Word in our hearts will carry us through everything we face. But at the same time, He isn't waiting to zap us because we didn't get up after a night of feedings, or just because we are exhausted from life. When you try to read at night and wake up with your face smushed into the pages, He understands.

If those times of the day aren't working for you, try having a "loud time" with God. Andrew Murray wrote, "It is when the soul is hushed in silent awe and worship . . . that the still small voice of the blessed Spirit will be heard." [2] He didn't say that everything else has to be quiet in order for our soul to be hushed before Him.

Think about it: Don't we want our children to see us spending time with the God who gives us strength? If we always spend quiet time with Him before they are awake or after they are sleeping soundly, they could miss seeing firsthand that He is our lifeline.

God says, "Your strength will come from settling down in complete dependence on me" (Isaiah 30:15 THE MESSAGE). I don't know about you, but it's hard for me to sit down once my kids are awake. For some reason we moms feel like we have to be "up and at 'em."

True, there are things that we have to do, but taking a break, resting with the Lord, listening to Him even when it's loud around us—those are the things that will carry us through all the remaining tasks and decisions the day holds.

Father, what a relief it is to me to know that you know right where I am. I can quit trying to impress you by my efforts and just rest in you, even if the moments are loud. I pray you'll help me focus on you as I quiet my soul during the day. Help me remember that the day is not lost just because I didn't wake up and immediately spend time with you. Remind me to stop throughout my day. I feel the urge to be "doing" when my kids are awake. Slow me down. Draw me to you.

I pray that you will fill me with your patience when my kids need me. If I have to get up and come back, you'll go with me and meet me again. If I have to get up and I can't come back, thank you for understanding. Feel free to speak to me through the day. I pray that you'll open my ears so that I can hear from you. Open my eyes so I can see what you want to show me. Loving you . . . I pray in Jesus' name, amen.

MAMA**DRAMA**

Try this: Set your kitchen timer to go off once every hour during the day—9:09, 10:10, 11:11, 12:12, 1:01, etc. When the beeper goes off, pray, read your Bible, or put on a praise CD. Some hours it probably won't work, but when it does, you'll be reminded to spend time with the Lord several times throughout the day, not just in the morning.

Praying and Listening

WHEN YOU THINK about praying, what comes to your mind? I've always thought of talking to God about what was going on in my life and the lives of those I love. I've had lists that I pray through, asking God to grant my requests.

Recently, though, I read an article about a prayer conversation that involved *listening* to God.[3] Imagine that . . . it's not all about what I have to say! God wants to be a part of the conversation too. In the article the guy would write down what he said to God and then write down any thoughts He had in response to his prayer.

How do you know if the thoughts you receive are from God? Ask two questions: Is it consistent with the Scriptures, and is it consistent with the character of God? I decided to try it one day before I began my work on this book. Rather than just coming to Him with a list, I came with a blank piece of paper. Here is what transpired in our conversation:

> *Me:* Good morning, Lord.
> *God:* Good morning. I love you. How are you?
> *Me:* I don't know. How am I?
> *God:* You are courageous.
> *Me:* Courageous? Oh, Lord, I feel so overwhelmed.
> *God:* I am here.
> *Me:* Thank you for being so faithful. I am here too. Forgive me for holding back. Please help the wall that goes up when I say, "Here am I," to go away. I want to believe with all of me that you are trustworthy.
> *God:* I am.
> *Me:* Thank you for the affirmation that I'm courageous! I want my courage and confidence to be based on you. Please lead me in that direction. Lord, will you pour into me about this book?
> *God:* Yes.
> *Me:* Lord, did we jump into writing this—
> *God:* No. It's my plan.
> *Me:* Help me, Lord. Anything else, Lord? What about my

family? I worry so much about one of my kids.

God: She is incredible.

Me: Isn't she? They all are. Open my eyes to see that every day and what you are doing in their hearts. And what about my husband? What should I be doing? (Pause) What should I pray for him?

God: Pray for His heart. I can take care of the rest.

It seemed odd to me at first, this kind of two-way conversation with God. But I was so blessed by my time with Him. It made me hopeful about the day ahead. So now it's a common practice for me. Some days there is nothing that I can discern coming from the Lord. On those days I praise Him, listen, talk to Him about my concerns, listen, and listen some more.

MAMA**DRAMA**

Why don't you try this now. . . .

Hello, Lord . . .

_____

_____

_____

Expecting Too Much

"Expectations:
(What) you hope someone will do
at a certain time,
in a certain place,
to a certain person,
in order to benefit you
in a certain way."[1]

The Good Ol' Days

SHARON AND I had an incredible childhood. We were blessed with a wonderful home and extraordinary parents. Sometimes we unintentionally put expectations on our husbands and children based on our past family experience. We feel that if our children aren't getting to live on a farm, have animals, milk a cow, and play in a hay barn (like we did), they'll be warped for life! You'd think having a good home life would be a great thing, but it can also have negative consequences. Allow me to share an early "marital growth spurt."

Several years ago my husband, Charles, and I were really struggling. We found ourselves at odds about everything. The main problem seemed to be communication. One conflict we were having had lasted off and on for two weeks. I was miserable. I longed for him to talk to me, and I was willing to try anything to make it happen.

I became so desperate to get some kind of response that I began making subtle but negative verbal jabs, just trying to evoke some kind of reaction. I didn't even care that he might blow up . . . I just wanted to know what was going on in his head. *At least he would be talking to me, even if he were yelling,* I thought.

It didn't work. He closed up even more. One night I broke down and cried. I told Charles that I was tired of feeling like this. Even as the tears dripped down my face, he remained silent and eventually fell asleep. I was so hurt. I also felt hopeless, like things would never change. The chasm between us grew wider.

Finally, one night after we went to bed, I tried to talk to him about it again. This time he listened, and when I paused, he responded, "I have two things to say: First, here's what was modeled for me. My dad was a rather private man—not very emotionally or spiritually expressive. So, my mom assumed the role of spiritual leader. Second, I am not going to be as expressive as your dad or your brother. I feel like you're expecting me to be like they are. I'm not."

I was stunned. I lay in silence as the tears began to fall down my cheeks. I had been feeling rejected by my husband's silence, and he was feeling scorned by my expectations. In that moment I realized that I had been placing unrealistic expectations on Charles.

I asked him for forgiveness. Then I began to tell him all of the reasons why I fell in love with him. It wasn't because he was like my dad. I fell in love with Charles because of who he was, and I loved him just the way he was. I knew that. I had just forgotten and I needed to be reminded.

Just as Charles' home life was all he had known, my home life was all I'd known. They were different. Some of you had a great childhood, like Sharon and me. You had great parents and you have wonderful memories. That should be a good thing, right? Well, it is a good thing—until we start to idealize or idolize our past, expecting those in our present life to re-create the "good ol' days."

A friend of ours told us something that her husband said: "Don't let the blessings of the past be stumbling blocks for today." Maybe that quote will hit you, as it did me . . . right where I needed it! I am learning to draw on the love of my childhood without lording it over my loved ones. God is teaching me to love the uniqueness of my past while experiencing the joy of the present.

With that thought in mind, ask yourself some questions. What are you holding on to? What unrealistic expectations are you dangling over those you love? Let go. If we don't, we'll never be able to see the blessings of today in those we love.

> *Lord, you know what my childhood was like. You know about all of the blessings and the bruises that those years left behind. Help me to yield the gift of my childhood to you. Please, Lord, don't let the memories, good or bad, haunt me. Help me to not dwell in the past too much, because I don't want to miss the blessings that you have for me in the present. Thank you for working through my past experiences to make me a better wife, mother, daughter, sister, and friend today. Amen.*

MAMA**DRAMA**

Write down a list of your five strongest expectations for your husband and your children. Prayerfully examine your list. Are your expectations fair, or are they unjust carry-overs from your childhood? Give your list to God and ask Him to help you see clearly which ones are valid and which ones are not fair to your loved ones.

Commit 1 Corinthians 13:4–5 to memory. "Love is patient, love is kind. It does not envy, it does not boast, it is not proud. It is not rude, it is not self-seeking, it is not easily angered, it keeps no record of wrongs." Meditate on these words and let them remind you to see your family the way He does.

A Fresh Start

J'VE HAD TO adopt my kids two times," she said with a smile. I looked at this mom a little confused, trying to think how she adopted them twice and why. As if to answer my questions she said, "I thought about how God has adopted us with our past and He starts working on things right where we are. He doesn't expect us to be perfect, but He takes us as we are. He doesn't give up on us."

She continued, "I realized that I was worrying about what I hadn't done raising my kids and was feeling horrible about it. So I called a family meeting, and I told them how I was going to follow God's lead—take them under my wing again at this stage of life and begin the parenting process afresh. I explained, 'If I adopted you today at your current ages, I would get you with all of your past—the good and the bad. I would do my best, starting now on the day of adoption. So starting now, I adopt you again, and these are the things I want to do differently from this point on.' This seemed to be the perfect solution to getting past my feelings of failure about the job I had been doing with them up to that point."

It's easy to fall into habits that eventually become a part of your family. Maybe the kids constantly interrupt your conversation or you've heard yourself speaking in ways that the children aren't allowed to speak. Maybe you are doing all the work without any help from your family, or you're all eating out constantly, running from here to there. Whatever your scenario, there are traps that all of us fall into, and sometimes we need a *fresh start*.

Instead of yelling and complaining, try restarting your family. That mom was letting her kids know that she was still glad to be their mom and hadn't given up on them. She was saying to them, "If I had to choose today, I'd still choose you."

Do you need to start over with your family? Do you feel like you *could* give up on them? (If so, don't worry—you're normal!) Maybe you need to get away by yourself or with your husband to think clearly about the trends in your family. When you get back, call a family meeting to introduce the new rules and new freedoms or to ask forgiveness for past mistakes. Then adopt them. Start over, with all of the past in the past. Today is a new day!

Lord, you were gracious beyond measure to adopt us into your family. You didn't ask us to clean up our act and then come to you, but you have taken us as we are. Thank you for giving us second, third, and fourth chances. . . . Help us do the same with our children. Show us things that we are allowing (or aren't allowing) in our home that we should change. Help us know when we should be more careful and when we should lighten up. Help us accept our kids just as they are. Refocus our minds. Restart us, Lord. We pray this in Jesus' name as your grateful adopted kids. Amen.

MAMA**DRAMA**

If it has been a while since you've been away by yourself or with your husband, take some time soon to go away and refocus. As you brainstorm about a better future, maybe these kinds of questions will be helpful to consider: What is the tone of our family; how do we speak to one another? Do our kids seem happy? If not, what might be the reason? Are there any underlying issues that need to be forgiven to restore family harmony? Where could we relax some things and where do they need to be tightened up?

Return to your children with fresh resolve to begin again in a spirit of love and acceptance. Make it an excuse to have a celebration, and expect God to do great things in every member of the family!

Set Free

EVERY DAY his mom and dad would badger him about his home-work. He didn't make bad grades, but they didn't trust him to get the work done on his own. Finally, in tenth grade he bluntly told them, "If you will leave me alone, I'll make better grades." His parents agreed to give it a try and watched as their son signed up for advanced courses and proceeded to maintain good grades.

As moms, we often feel like that tied-down teenager, only we're tied down by our own expectations. A grandma told me that when her kids were little, she had in her mind what her life should be like. So she stayed up until three o'clock in the morning sewing the costumes, baking cookies, cleaning, and catching up on laun-dry.

After several years at this pace, she had a nervous breakdown. She said that she missed so much of her children's growing up because she was trying to be the perfect mom. She was more con-cerned about "doing" than "being." (She said she has learned her lesson and spends as much time as she can with her grandchil-dren.)

One mom told me, "As hard as you thought it would be to be a mom, it's that much harder. You wish it could be only as hard as what you thought it would be!" Maybe we had those unrealistic ideas before we had kids, but now that they are here, it's okay to let go of some of the expectations we have of ourselves and how we thought life would be.

Galatians 5:1 says, "It is for freedom that Christ has set us free. Stand firm, then, and do not let yourselves be burdened again by a yoke of slavery." Like the teenager given the freedom to do what he could do without the "slavery" his parents had hung around his neck, Jesus can do the same for us. He can take the burdens and expectations that hang around our necks, weigh-ing us down, and give us instead the freedom to be what He made us to be.

Focus your eyes on that freedom. Ask God to open your heart

and mind to really accept His freedom from all you've expected of yourself. He will strengthen you, enabling you to not just do your best, but also do your best while He holds you up and cheers you on.

Have you been bogged down about your "home work"? Then cut yourself some slack. Our load as moms is heavy enough as it is. Don't add more than you need to carry. Identify the expectations that are enslaving you. Then give them to the Lord and see what He can do. Instead of being paralyzed by guilt, you'll come alive as the mom God intended you to be. He has set you free, so live that way!

Lord, you know us better than we know ourselves. Sometimes we don't even know what expectations we have of ourselves. We just know that we are running around frustrated and overwhelmed with too much to do. Show us as we go through our daily life what things we can let go of, what things don't really matter and are not ours to control. Help us, Lord, to stop badgering ourselves about all that we "should" be doing; help us to slow down so we can enjoy our families and just "be" with them. Thankful to be free, I pray this in Jesus' name. Amen.

MAMA**DRAMA**

Think about your day today. What could you let go of to make your day more about what God wants to do than about what you expect of yourself?

Make a list of the things that you expect of yourself. Look up the word *free* and any forms of that word in the concordance of your Bible. Meditate on those verses and ask God to help you live in the freedom that He has given you through Jesus.

Don't Dwell on It—
Just Passing Through

AS MY SISTER-IN-LAW was reading a book to my girls, she came across the line "Don't dwell on it." Crislynn stopped her and said, "What does 'dwell' mean?" Brittlea, my eight-year-old, piped up, "It's where you live." At first we thought her definition didn't fit the context of the sentence, but the more we considered it, we realized it fit perfectly.

Sometimes my kids will confess things they are thinking if they feel guilty for their thoughts. I tell them that just because they have a bad thought or idea doesn't mean they have sinned. Just as we don't intend to let a fly into our house, thoughts can loom at the door of our minds and enter without invitation. It's when we don't do anything to rid ourselves of the pesky thought that it becomes sin.

I believed my kids were the ones who needed to hear this advice as they struggled with thoughts that made them feel guilty. However, as Laurie and I talked one day, she said, "Sharon, we're doing the same thing. We're beating ourselves up for things we *think*. Maybe I am about to blow up inside, making me feel guilty, but when I don't blow up I'm exercising self-control—and that's something I can feel good about."

As moms, it's easy for us to be hard on ourselves, feeling guilty for things that were *only* thoughts. But we need to remember something: If we didn't stop there, unload, and hang pictures on the wall, we haven't done anything wrong. It's when we dwell there that we run into problems.

In 2 Corinthians 10:5 it says, "We take captive every thought to make it obedient to Christ." That's how we fight the tendency to dwell on things that take our eyes off of the Lord. When the thoughts come, take them to the Lord and get rid of the ones that don't match His character.

If you are dwelling on something you said to your kids (maybe you jumped all over them for swinging and bruising the grocery bag full of fresh fruit), ask forgiveness from God and your kids—then move on. When you feel guilty for your harsh words again, don't start building a house around that thought; rather, shoo it out the door of your mind because you have been forgiven.

If you are having silent conversations with your husband because he left his clothes out again, take the thought captive, and tear down the walls that have started going up by praying for him as you put the lost clothes where they belong. If you're feeling guilty for the actions of your children (such as when they fuss about anything and everything), pray for them and discipline when you need to, but remember: We are all responsible for our own actions, not the actions of others (including our children).

Where have you been dwelling today? Where will you live for the rest of today? The good news is, you have a choice. When those thoughts sneak into your mind, take them captive. Don't dwell there. No one wants to live in that neighborhood!

> *Lord, you know the thoughts that are common to my mind. Help me to not feel guilty for things I think that I immediately push out of my thoughts. And help me identify those things that I am dwelling on that have already begun to build walls—walls that need to be torn down. One day spent in your house beats thousands spent elsewhere. I'd rather scrub floors in the house of my God than be honored as a guest in the palace of sin (Psalm 84:10). Open my eyes when I'm living somewhere other than with you. How lovely is your dwelling place! Dwelling on you, in Jesus' name, amen.*

MAMA**DRAMA**

Make a quick list of the negative things you have a tendency to dwell on. Commit the list to God, asking Him to help you notice when you begin to make yourself at home in those ungodly places.

The Handprint

THE GIRLS WERE so excited! We were finally going to paint their room. We were doing our own episode of the "complete room makeover." All the furniture was moved away from the walls and the plastic drop cloth was in place. Of course I was going to be a "good" mom and let my three children—ages three, six, and eight—help.

I began with the oldest. Alec did pretty well keeping most of the paint on the wall. Only a little got on his elbow when he accidentally bumped the wet paint. Next came the six-year-old. Tripping over the drop cloth as she entered the room, Abby caught herself between the wall and dresser. She already had paint down one side of her body, and she hadn't even begun painting.

Frustrated by her clumsiness, I scolded, "Be careful, honey! You are going to get paint everywhere!" Apologizing, she stood at attention, waiting for her orders. Providing her with specific instructions, I handed over the paint roller.

She was a little surprised that it was more challenging than she'd anticipated. However, she was determined; she rolled most of the paint out of the roller. As she refilled her roller with paint, it seemed to have a leak at one end. It dripped down the roller, missing the paint pan (of course), and fell on the drop cloth.

She looked up at me with an "oops" look on her face. With little patience, I responded, "Don't step in it or you'll track it all over the house!" She *finally* finished her section of the wall, and now it was the three-year-old daughter's turn. (What was I thinking?) I wiped my brow and sighed with exasperation. I tried my best to put on a "happy face" as my littlest bounced toward the room. She had been waiting patiently for "her turn."

As she walked in the door, she leaned in one direction to step around the furniture. As she did, she put her hand on the wall to brace herself. Immediately she removed her hand and looked at me with a stunned expression. "Avery, honey," I said, "you can't touch the wall. Remember, it's wet." I looked around for something to clean her hand, but found nothing. I pulled at my shirt. "Here, wipe your hands on this." I said. She apologized profusely as she excitedly approached the painting pan. I handed her the paint roller, and she did her best to get most of the paint on the wall.

She was doing great until she got off balance and leaned into the wall. Again, she forgot and caught herself with her hand. Suddenly I felt all the patience drain from my body. I had none left. I raised my voice impatiently: "Avery, don't touch the wall!"

Disappointed in herself, she looked up at me with her big blue eyes and said, "I'm sorry, Mommy. I didn't mean to." I told her it was okay, and she wiped her hand on my shirt once again. I convinced her that Mommy could finish the rest.

Several days after finishing the project, I was unloading the dryer. As I began folding the clothes, I pulled my old paint shirt from the pile. I was shocked when I saw it. There on the front of my shirt was a perfect little green handprint. Tears welled up in my eyes as I gazed at it. You see, I had been so worried about getting the job done "right" that I had forgotten to focus on what was important—enjoying the journey with my precious children.

Now, every time I see that shirt, I am thankful that Avery fell into the paint that day. If she hadn't, I wouldn't have such a vivid reminder of how precious life is!

Lord, help me to remember that being a parent is a privilege, not a punishment. Please don't let the weight of my daily responsibilities rob me of my sense of wonder. Remind me that the children you have placed in my care are as individually unique as their handprints. I thank you, Lord, for each of my children, and I am grateful that you've given them to me. Amen.

MAMA**DRAMA**

Start today and make a handprint of each of your children. Each year make another one and place it in a keepsake box. It's amazing to see how they grow.

When you give gifts to grandparents, use your kids' handprints on the gift so that it has that personal touch only they can give.

Contentment—
It's Your Choice

These days are here, these days are now.
Help us treasure every day somehow.
Don't look back or up ahead, but
live and love today.
These days are here and then they're gone,
Help us be content; they won't last long,
For we only have these days.

Words by Laurie Hilliard
Music by Pat and Sharon Autry

Wastin' Wishes

WHEN MY HUSBAND was a kid, he would wish for things he couldn't have or didn't need—like a new bike, a designer shirt, or staying up an extra thirty minutes—and his mom would say, "You're wastin' wishes." It annoyed him then, but he has since realized that wasting wishes means wasting your time. When we are always wanting *more,* we miss out on what we *have.*

It's easy to be distracted by all the stuff. I don't necessarily want a new house, but you can bet that I want the house we have to be clean (wish #1) and I'd like it to be decorated as perfectly as the houses on HGTV (wish #2). I can wish for more money (#3) to use for decorating and maybe even some landscaping out front (#4). I can look at the clothes someone else is wearing and wish for a new wardrobe (#5). When I pull up beside a shiny SUV in my dirty van with the bumper falling off and a missing hubcap, I can feel poor and wish we could buy a fancy new vehicle (wish #6).

Our wishes could go on and on, couldn't they? Having an SUV or a landscaped yard aren't bad things. But when I'm disgruntled because our neighbor's yard looks great or I'm embarrassed to pull my vehicle out of my garage, those wishes rob me of both my time and my joy.

Have you ever been caught in the trap of wishing for things that you don't really need and can't afford? Have you found yourself irritated, finding that the source of your unhappiness is rooted in wishing for things to be different? Talk about wastin' wishes!

Again, it's not that having nice things or going shopping are bad things. It's when the nice things consume our thoughts and emotions and get in front of our relationship with God that they become a problem. When we are caught up in the stuff, we miss the joy. Proverbs 13:7 puts our wishes and wanting more in perspective: "A pretentious, showy life is an empty life; a plain and simple life is a full life" (THE MESSAGE).

Luke 12:15 warns us to "Watch out! Be on your guard against all kinds of greed; a man's life does not consist in the abundance of his possessions" (or the school his child attends, or the job he holds). I have often told my children that we might not be rich in money, but we are rich in relationships—with God and one another. They believe it and have reminded me on my "wastin' wishes" days that we are rich because we have "the coolest family in the world."

We've all been guilty of comparing what we have with what others have. It is a trap. Don't fall for it today. When you catch yourself wishing for things to be different, stop and say thank you for what you *do* have. You are worth far more than the abundance of your possessions. When you are wishing for more things, remember that a showy life is an empty life. Instead, focus on being "rich toward God" (Luke 12:21 THE MESSAGE). We've been given so much. How could we waste wishes, wishin' for more?

Lord, our society is filled with things we "need." Sometimes it's hard to distinguish between what we really need and what we want. Please help us focus on what you have for us. When our eyes become distracted by "stuff" or another family who seems to have it better than we do, remind us that we are rich because of our relationship with you. Our family members alone represent wealth beyond measure. Help us to be on guard against all kinds of greed. Thank you for not counting our worth by our possessions. Teach us not to fight having a plain and simple life but to value that simplicity. Wishin' for all you have for us, we pray this in Jesus' name. Amen.

MAMA**DRAMA**

As a family, make a list of all the things for which you are thankful (examples: a dishwasher, towels, a house, Mom, Dad, Jesus, the Bible, a pet, clothes, etc.). List as many things as you can think of. Then take turns crossing off things that you could live without. Pray together, thanking God for blessing you with so much and making you rich because you have Him and one another.[1]

Living the Dream

T HIS MORNING I had lofty hopes of getting away from the
house early to find a peaceful place to write. As I was trying
to finish drying my hair, I realized my best intentions were being
thwarted by a crying baby who didn't want to take his nap and a
wailing child who had a boo-boo that needed to be kissed. *Why
does it take me so long to get out of here?* I thought, concluding
that I wasn't going to be getting *anywhere* very fast today.

In that moment my mind drifted to a beautiful, quiet, scenic
place—a place of calm serenity. I was picturing a place with a
covered back porch overlooking a pond surrounded by trees. The
porch would be adorned with wicker furniture accented by beautiful antique quilts. I imagined the birds singing and the sun
glistening through the green leaves of the hovering trees as
Tchaikovsky played in the background. And I . . . I would be overlooking it all, laptop in hand, recording the inspiration as it
poured through my fingers. Oh, and I would also be sipping a
cup of hot cappuccino!

I thought, *If only I had a place like that, I'm sure I'd have no
trouble finding inspiration to write.* Then another notion came to
me: *You know, I'll bet if my house were cleaner, my mind wouldn't
be so cluttered, muddling the few creative ideas I might have. And
I know I would be able to think more clearly if my children
wouldn't interrupt my thought processes all the time. The inspira-
tional thoughts would just flow from my pen.*

Jolted back to reality by a baby who was *still* crying, I almost
chuckled out loud at the silly thoughts I was having. What I was
wanting was not reality; it was an unrealistic dream, an unattaina-
ble ideal. A life with no interruptions, no distractions, and no clut-
ter meant a life with no children! What was I thinking? If I had
all that, I'd have no family. If I had no family, I'd have no inspiration for stories. If I had no stories, I'd have no reason to write.

I realized in that moment that the dream is not "out there"
somewhere. It is right here. It is right now. *I'm living the dream.*

As moms, it is easy for us to long for something "out there" to make us happy, bring fulfillment, and create contentment. We think, *If only I could have a new car, or a different house, then I'd be content.* Or maybe we believe, *If my baby would sleep as long as hers, or if my husband were more supportive, then I would never complain again!* Yeah, right! Who are we trying to fool? So many times I *miss* the dream I'm living because I'm looking "out there" for something else to satisfy me.

The baby finally went to sleep. I eventually got my hair dried, and the boo-boo was better (for the moment). But before I left the house to go write, I just happened to look out my dirty window. I stood there for a few moments as tears began to well up in my eyes. I watched my imperfect kids, with mismatched clothes on, playing (and arguing) . . . and I smiled.

I *was* living the dream. And I had almost missed it. So in that moment I thanked God for the dream I'd been given to live. If this is a dream, I don't want to wake up!

> *Father, thank you for the dream you're allowing me to live. Forgive me when I miss the blessings of today because I'm longing for tomorrow. Lord, I don't want to focus so much on the task at hand that I can't enjoy the process. Help me walk a little slower, hug a little tighter, and gaze a little longer. Thank you for today. Amen.*

MAMA**DRAMA**

Try walking slower today. Don't drag your kids—their legs are much shorter than yours. Go at their pace.

Give your kids a hug when they didn't ask for it. Ask them, "Do you know how glad I am to be your mom?"

These Days

SHARON AND I were blessed to have an amazing mom. She was (and still is) our number one cheerleader! She came to every game we played, attended every band concert, and happily transported us to every practice. We knew she would always be there for us. But there was something else she did that I'll never forget. It was something she said to us over and over.

I remember her telling us, as we were growing up, how much she enjoyed each stage of our lives. I don't remember her ever wishing us to be any age other than the age we were. She would say things like, "You guys are so much fun. I can't imagine it getting any better." Then we'd get a little older and she would tell us again, "You know, I think *this* stage has got to be the best. I can't imagine it getting any better." But I always knew that it would! Now she thinks having grandchildren is pretty grand—imagine that!

Interestingly enough, Mom would not save these comments for special occasions; she would remind us of her contentedness in the daily routines of life. While washing dishes, doing laundry, or taking out the trash she reminded us, right then and there, of how much she loved her life with us. Not only did it change our perspective but it probably changed hers too. She lived Ephesians 5:15–16: "Be very careful, then, how you live —not as unwise but as wise, making the most of every opportunity."

Over and over through the years, Mom encouraged us by telling us how much she loved being our mom right where we were. She didn't dwell on how wonderful we were when we were little, nor was she always dreaming of what tomorrow held for us. She enjoyed the moment.

What a gift she gave us! Mom inspired us to "live and love today . . . because we only have *these days.*" I wrote the lyrics to this song because of her!

"These Days"

I've heard it said a hundred times "Enjoy it while it lasts!"
They say these days will come and go and then they'll be
 the past.
I know it's true, they'll grow up soon; how can I make it
 last?
These days slip by too fast.

My mom she always tells me "As each day passes by,
Your love will grow just like they do—a fact you can't deny.
Though these toddling legs bring joy your heart has never
 known,
Think how much you will love when they're grown!"

These days are here, these days are now.
Help us treasure every day somehow.
Don't look back or up ahead, but live and love today.
These days are here, and then they're gone.
Help us be content; they won't last long,
For we only have these days.

I know I shouldn't worry what the future has in store.
He cares for birds, so I know He cares for my children so
 much more.
You tell me not to fret, but simply put my trust in you.
In these days you'll see them through.

These days are here, these days are now.
Help us treasure every day somehow.
Don't look back or up ahead, but live and love today.
These days are here, and then they're gone.
Help us be content; they won't last long,
For we only have these days.

Words by Laurie Hilliard
Music by Pat and Sharon Autry

*Father, today is a gift. Thank you for the reminder to enjoy
the moment. Help me to not worry about tomorrow but to live
and love this very day, trusting you to see us through. Remind
me to tell my children how glad I am to be their mom, so that
they'll never doubt my love for them, or yours. Amen.*

MAMA**DRAMA**

When you tuck your kids into bed tonight (no matter what their age), whisper in their ear, "You are my favorite little boy/girl in the whole world." (If you have more than one child of the same sex, you might say, "You are my favorite eleven-year-old boy in the whole world.")

A Thankful Heart
Is a Happy Heart

HAVE YOU EVER watched "Madame Blueberry," a *VeggieTales* movie? We've watched it many times for a reason. You see, it is my husband's prescription for an ungrateful attitude displayed by our children. When he sees a pouty lip sticking out or hears a whiny "I wish I had a (bike, dress, ball, toy, computer game, etc.) like they do," he prescribes one viewing of "Madame Blueberry."

This chubby little blueberry is blessed to have friends who bear with her, a great tree house (in VeggieTale World, tree houses are higher class than homes built on the ground), and lots of fun stuff. But she can't see any of her blessings because she is blindly consumed by what she doesn't have. She is "blue" with envy!

When given a showy invitation to the "Stuff Mart," she accepts it and proceeds to buy one of everything. On the way, she meets a couple of remarkable children. One is happy just having her family there for her birthday, even though she isn't receiving any gifts. The other is sad for a moment when his dad tells him they can't afford the train set, but then he accepts it and moves on.

She is stunned by the gratefulness of these children and their ability to keep a smile on their faces even when they didn't get any stuff. You'll have to watch it to know the ending, but without ruining it for you, Madame Blueberry finally realizes that *a thankful heart is a happy heart.*

Unfortunately, I'm afraid that I can relate all too well to Madame Blueberry. You probably can too. It's easy to look at the home of a friend and decide you couldn't possibly invite her to your house because it isn't as classy or as put together as hers. Or we can look at how others dress and decide we must go shopping . . . ASAP.

Maybe your friend's children are more polite than your kids. So the next day, you make a whole new list of rules and spring them on your unknowing children. It could be that another husband treats his wife more lovingly, and you let the thought run through your mind that you are married to a clod. All of these thoughts are based on what someone else has that we wish we had. During those times of wanting, the cure is to remember that *a thankful heart is a happy heart.*

I often think that thankfulness is reserved for writing thank-you notes and for that one time of year when we have lots of turkey and too much dessert. But *every day* is an occasion for gratefulness. As mentioned in an earlier devotional, a thankful heart can change your whole perspective. Does it mean that we ignore the struggles in life and put on a happy face all the time? God's Word says it so clearly in Philippians 4:6: "Do not worry about anything, but pray and ask God for everything you need, always giving thanks" (NCV).

Why should we give thanks along with our requests? Because God knows our tendency to focus on our own needs and wants. If we pray only about the things we "need," the list becomes quite selfish. But when we cover all of our requests with thanks for what we already have, it doesn't put so much emphasis on our desires.

So in the good times and the bad, thank Him. Along with your requests, worries, and fears, remember to count your blessings as well, because a thankful heart really is a happy heart.

> *Lord, you know our tendency as women to look at the lives of others and throw a pity party for ourselves because our life doesn't appear to be as rosy as theirs. Forgive us, Lord, for assuming that others don't have struggles. Help us to see their hearts instead of only seeing our wants. Remind us to be thankful for all you have done for us. You have blessed us in so many ways; help us see all of them. Thank you for Jesus. It's because of Him that we even have the ability to bring our requests to you. We pray this in His name, amen.*

MAMA**DRAMA**

Get a copy of "Madame Blueberry" (if you don't own one, borrow from a friend or your church library) and watch it with your kids today. When you are tempted to get stuck wanting things that others have, ask God for what you *need,* then thank Him for the blessings in your life.

Gifts Come in
All Shapes and Sizes

I'LL NEVER FORGET the time my daughter (who is always bringing us little gifts) came around the kitchen counter with
sparkly eyes, hands behind her back, and exclaimed, "Mom, you
are going to be so excited about what I found!"

She handed me her "gift" wrapped in a dish towel and secured
by a hair bow. I carefully opened the present and found her once-
lost but now-found Care Bear panties! Her face gleamed as she
waited for my reaction. I hugged her, thrilled with the item, but I
was even more elated to have *her* as a gift.

When you and I choose a gift for someone, we are careful to
pick out something they would like. We put some thought into
their preferences and look for the perfect item that says, "I know
you and I love you." We wrap it with pretty paper, a bow, and a
card, letting them know who gave the gift and that we treasure
them. Then we wait as they open other presents and finally come
to the one that is so familiar. Don't you get excited about someone opening the gift you gave them? I do.

Our children are a *gift from God* that says, "I know you and I
love you." Psalm 127:3 says, "Children are a gift from the Lord; they
are a reward from him" (NLT). Each child comes with different wrapping—hair, height, eye color, and skin tone—and what's inside is
always a surprise! They may be quiet thinkers or social butterflies,
nosy Noras or shy sweethearts, grumpy goats or happy hearted, con-
tented or demanding, busy or carefree, scatterbrained or organized,
jungle babies or calm "aaaaah" kids, brainy or a little bit ditzy!

From an all-knowing heart, God has carefully chosen our children for us with all their decorative personalities. They aren't perfect. Neither are we. But God put us together. We are the ones for
them. They are the kids for us.

It's easy to question His choice at times because you and I can
be the complete opposite personality of our children. We sometimes clash and have trouble figuring each other out. But God
knew that if our kids were just like us, we would not need His
help. When you are suffering from the common "I don't like my

child today" syndrome (it's normal), look to God as the only cure. Let it be a reminder that you need Him.

Tell your kids as you go through your day that they are a gift from God. And when you are praying together with them, remember to thank God for putting you together. You won't always agree with your kids. You may question His purpose. But you can both be confident that God had a plan in putting you together.

> *Lord, I am grateful for the kids you've given me, but I have questioned your plan at times. I want to be the mom they need, but sometimes I feel like we are complete opposites. This makes it hard for me to see their strengths. It's easier for me to get hung up on their faults. You are perfect. You didn't make a mistake when you wrapped the individual packages of my children and sent them to me. Help me see deeper than the things that bother me.*
>
> *Draw me closer to you as I seek your wisdom in dealing with my children. Thank you, Lord, for your precious gifts! Gratefully I pray in Jesus' name, amen.*

MAMA**DRAMA**

(Note: This activity is a great one, but it takes some time and planning. If you don't have time right now, store it away for another time—maybe when your kids are a little older. I'm using it on their tenth birthdays.)

Choose a special gift for your child. Pick out wrapping paper that reminds you of them. Then take some time with them (individually) and tell them that you have chosen a special gift just for them. Explain that just as you chose a gift, God gave them special gifts inside . . . like their personalities, ideas, talents, and character. Acknowledge special qualities they have, like honesty, gentleness, caring, helpfulness, etc.

Talk about their outer qualities in an encouraging way, but keep the focus on their inner qualities. Then let them open the gift. Try not to be discouraged if your child seems distracted or not as excited about the gift as you had hoped. Part of the purpose in this activity is to remind you of the blessing and God-given gift you have living in your home.

Livin' It

"Love the Lord your God with all your heart,
all your soul,
and all your strength.
Always remember these commands I give you today.
Teach them to your children, and talk about them
when you sit at home
and walk along the road,
when you lie down
and when you get up."

Deuteronomy 6:5–7 (NCV)

Let Your Light So Shine

"THIS LITTLE LIGHT of mine, I'm gonna let it shine . . ." You've probably heard the song. It's based on Matthew 5:16: "Let your light shine before men, that they may see your good deeds and praise your Father in heaven." Even though it is a familiar verse, sometimes we read Scripture passages with fresh eyes when God's Spirit brings their truth home to us. This happened to me one day as I read this verse in Matthew.

I thought about the difference it would make in my home if I let the light of Jesus shine through me. What would it be like for my husband and kids to see my good works as deeds done to glorify the Lord? I thought about the verse for several days after, and I found that I was handling situations differently because *I wanted to live it out* in a tangible way.

Fast forward one week.

Laurie and I were sitting together, waiting to go on stage to speak, when a sweet lady took the microphone and read the same verse, "Let your light shine. . . ." As she began praying, I also prayed, *Lord, I commit to let my light shine with my family today.* Knowing the day I had before me, I knew this would be a challenge, but I knew that with His strength it was possible. We had four hundred miles to drive that day with three children, but the prospects were promising. We were driving in our bus, which was equipped with games, a TV, books, and food—lots of food.

The trip started and things were going fine in the beginning. There is one thing you should understand: because the bus moves around a lot, it's important to "tie everything down." Every time the wheels start rolling, we latch drawers, cabinets, doors, and the refrigerator . . . especially the refrigerator.

Along the way we stopped at a favorite spot for all of us, QT (QuikTrip), to get a great fountain drink. During our stop someone unlatched the fridge, and in my excitement over my cherry vanilla Diet Coke, I forgot to re-latch it. We turned to the right to enter the freeway when my husband misjudged a little and ran over a curb, jolting everything to the left. Not latching the fridge and running over a curb . . . that's a bad combination! The door swung open and I watched in horror as apple juice, milk, white bean soup, Cokes, ketchup, and anything else that was loose literally flew from the shelves. Each landed with a crash, a splat, or a spew. I could do nothing about it, lest I get hit in the head by a jar of flying sweet-pickle relish. (Sweet means sticky!)

As the scene progressed, I finally closed and latched the door. I sighed as I assessed the damage. This was by far the worst spill we had ever had in our bus. I had always been so thankful for a full-sized refrigerator in our bus . . . until now!

In my mind, all I could think was, *"Let your light shine before men, that they may see your good deeds and praise your Father in heaven."* I wanted to scream, but I didn't. I wanted to accuse my husband for driving carelessly, but I didn't. I wanted to yell at my children to stay out of the mess . . . Okay . . . I did speak firmly, but I didn't yell.

So as we continued down the road (there was no place to stop), I squished through the mess to the back of the bus, prayed, then put a smile on my face and made my way to the front of the bus. Six little eyes, along with my husband looking in the rearview mirror, waited to see how I would respond. I said, "Well, our floor needed to be cleaned anyway!" Only God could do that—to Him be the glory!

Dear Father, you are amazingly patient with us. I'm realizing that your gift of children and the circumstances of life are probably going to grow that patience in me. I pray that my words and actions in the midst of a crisis, however big or small, will be less reactive and more resolved to treat those I love with respect. Help me to let my light shine before my family, so they can see that the good deeds I do are for your glory. On my own I can't shine, but you can shine through me. I commit myself again to you, in Jesus' name. Amen.

MAMA**DRAMA**

Sing "This Little Light of Mine" with your kids. Maybe it will be one of those tunes that gets stuck in your head so you'll be reminded through your day to let your light shine for the Lord.

Now Is the Time

WHEN I WAS nineteen I found myself in a waiting room, flipping through magazines. When I stumbled on to a magazine with tons of ideas to make life more fun with your family, I was immediately drawn to it. I began subscribing to it at that time and continue to subscribe twelve years later.

As soon as I began receiving the magazines, I started a filing system where I could put the articles I would someday use with my family. In my idealistic mind, I envisioned all the great things I would do with my kids. Along with these fun ideas, I planned to have my children quoting books out of the Bible (instead of just verses). I was determined!

Three years later I married, and after three more years we began our family. I was thrilled to be a mom. Now was the time! Only, my baby girl was a little young to make crayon melts. A couple of years later I realized that it was finally "the time," but my life was so much more hectic by then. My daughter took lots of my time, plus I had added another child. My husband also needed my time. My friends needed me and I needed them. When was I supposed to fit in these mounds of great ideas I had stored away, or teach all those verses I longed for my kids to know?

I found myself discouraged, unmotivated, and too tired to do all those fun things I had dreamed of doing. Now, many years later, I've done a few things and taught some Scripture, but I've not been as serious about it as I once thought I would be.

Looking back, I realize that when I was nineteen, I had no experience at *being* a mother. It looked so fun, so concrete, so "easy." (How could I have ever thought that?) Now that I am experienced at being a mom and know it's not always a thrill, I've come to realize that it's definitely not a cut-and-dried job, and not even close to "easy."

But my dreams of sharing fun times with my children and teaching them Scripture and the truths of God were not in vain. God put those desires in me. Like anything worthwhile, they don't come easy. But they are so rewarding when they work out. What I idealistically dreamed about at nineteen boils down to a lot of work, and my expectations were out of whack. However, I also know that whatever I am going to do with my kids, *now* is the time!

So how do I work with my schedule, my lack of energy, and my life as it is? Here are some of my thoughts:

1. I have to stop dreaming about tomorrow, or I'll miss today. Before I know it, I'll be wishing for grandkids and dreaming of what I'll do with them!

2. I'll use the little moments along the way—bath time, breakfast, in the car, before bed. (Deuteronomy 6:7)

3. I'll do fun things (goodness knows I have enough ideas), but not every day or even every week. I'll do what I can when I can.

4. I won't let myself be so busy with other things that I don't have time to do creative or really important things with my family. (If you're a single mom, military mom, or have a husband who works a lot, this one is harder for you. Give yourself the grace to do what you can.)

I realize that I need to surrender my idealistic view of being the best organized, most creative, and godliest woman in America! It's just not possible. But God knew I could be a great mom for my children. I trust Him now for the energy, creativity, and insight to be what He wants me to be.

Lord, I can put so much pressure on myself to be the "perfect" mom—the mom I thought I would be. Show me what is realistic for my life. Please take away the guilt that I often feel, and show me how to use the little moments. Show me the "fun things" you want me to do with my kids. I don't have to do everything, or even as much as my friend does with her children. Give me the energy and creativity to pour into my children the things that are so important, like your Word. Forgive me for being too hard on myself. You aren't nearly as demanding of me. Thank you for your grace. In Jesus' name I pray, amen.

MAMA**DRAMA**

Let your young kids use the rags in the bathtub to put on a bath-time puppet show. Matthew 8:23–27 is a good story to act out. Be ready for lots of splashing! The story of Jonah and the whale is also fun.

Once you have picked some age-appropriate Scriptures or activities, write them on your calendar. You probably won't memorize all the Scripture or do all the things recorded on the exact day that you listed it, but you'll be much more likely to remember it if it's in front of you. (For great ideas, check out: *www.familyfun.com.*)

Sometimes Being "Needy" Is a Good Thing

MY LITTLE GIRL Avery, who is five, has been sick for a week. She feels downright rotten—croup, sore throat, earache, and chills . . . the whole shebang! As her fever rises, her eyes tell me the result before the thermometer does. You probably know the signs because you've seen it in the eyes of your own child.

I've been doing everything I know to do for her, giving pain medicine as often as possible, but it doesn't seem to be helping much. To this medicinal ritual I have added an antibiotic, as well as cough syrup. It has been a long, challenging week. She feels awful and I'm beat! Between her not sleeping well, and a baby who doesn't yet sleep through the night, I'm pretty wiped out!

Ever since she came down with this, it seems she can only be consoled by my presence. It's not enough that I'm merely in the room; I must be near her, holding her. Yesterday afternoon, exhausted from the fever and infection in her body, she finally fell asleep on the couch. I was so thankful . . . for her and for me! She could rest and I was able to sneak away from her side to quickly tend to a few overdue chores that were piling up.

Just as I was beginning to feel a sense of accomplishment and freedom, she prematurely awakened with a horrible "barking" cough and a plugged-up nose. Blurry-eyed, she gasped for air as tears began to run down her cheeks. Fear gripped her little body. I quickly rushed to her side and wrapped my arms around her. She sobbed, "I needed you, Mommy." I squeezed her tightly and responded, "And Mommy was here, wasn't she?"

"But what if I needed you and you were gone?" she asked. I assured her that I was not going anywhere while she was so sick. Later that afternoon, I realized what had provoked such a question. When she was experiencing a drug-induced feeling of well-being (ibuprofen is a wonderful drug, isn't it?), she made a startling statement. Her big blue eyes looked up at me and penetrated deep into my heart. "Mommy," she said, "I'm sorry that you are not getting any writing done because I'm sick."

You see, prior to her becoming ill, I had been spending much of my time trying to meet a fast-approaching writing deadline. Everyone in the house knew Mom was constantly working on the book. After hearing her revealing statement, I immediately stopped what I was doing. I knelt down in front of her, looked into her eyes, took her face into my hands, and resolutely declared, "Sweetheart, I am doing what I *want* to be doing right now. You are *most* important to me. Don't you worry about the book; it will get done. Mommy is not worried about it. All I'm concerned about is you getting better. I know you need me right now and I am going to *be here!*"

Just as Avery desperately needed me when she was fearful, so am I in need of my heavenly Father. As a mom, I have a tendency to try to be independent and handle things on my own. However, it usually doesn't take long for me to realize how desperately I need Christ in my life. I love the familiar words to an old hymn called "I Need Thee Every Hour."

> I need thee every hour, Most gracious Lord;
> No tender voice like Thine, Can peace afford.
> I need Thee, oh, I need Thee; Every hour I need Thee!
> Oh, bless me now, my Savior, I come to Thee.
>
> Music by Robert Lowry (1826–1899), words by Annie S. Hawks (1835–1918)

Heavenly Father, I need you—not only every hour, but every moment. I confess that I often try to live this life all on my own. I act as if I can keep it all together, when inside I feel like I'm falling apart. I don't want to do it alone anymore. I need you. Thank you for being so faithful, for being right there whenever I call on you. Oh bless me now, my Savior—I come to Thee. Amen.

MAMA**DRAMA**

As you finish your quiet time today, sing the hymn quoted above. If you are not familiar with it, just speak it as a poem. Let God fill you with His presence.

A Gentle Answer Turns Away Wrath

W HY HAVEN'T YOU picked up your clothes off the floor?" I questioned, irritated by Alec's lack of response. "I've already asked you three times." He quickly replied, "But I didn't hear you." To which I immediately countered, "That's because you're *not listening*. You never hear anything I say when you're playing video games. How long have you been playing, anyway? Isn't your allotted time up?"

Or maybe this scenario is more familiar to you.

> *Mom:* "Girls, stop arguing!"
> *Older daughter:* "But, Mommy, I'm just trying to show her something, and she won't listen."
> *Younger daughter:* "But I had it first, and she's trying to take it away!"
> *Mom:* "Okay, I've had enough" (said as I stomp into the room). "I don't want to hear another word out of either one of you! If you can't share the toy, then neither of you will play with it. Go to your rooms!"

As Abby and Avery escape to their rooms, I follow them with one last criticism, "Why do you have to be so ugly to each other?"

Sound familiar? Maybe you need to change the gender of the child or the details of the situation slightly, but our reaction is many times the same. We lose it with our kids. Why is it so easy to talk so ugly to our kids when we would never speak to anyone else in such a manner?

You might be thinking, *It's because they know just how to push my buttons* (the button marked *Make Mom Lose Control*). I know I've had similar feelings, such as, *It's their fault. They deserve it. They made me mad!* But let's think about this. Is our reaction really *their* fault? And if it is a "right" reaction, then why do we feel so guilty?

After a morning of constantly picking on one of my children, I found myself feeling very defeated, guilty, and frustrated. I went to God, pleading with Him to work on my child's heart. Then, almost as an afterthought, I prayed, "Lord, show me what you want from me today." I was surprised when Proverbs 15:1 immediately popped into my mind. It says, "A gentle answer turns away wrath, but a harsh word stirs up anger."

That was the answer! It wasn't my child that God wanted to speak to that day . . . it was me! When I respond with a gentle answer, it serves to not only calm my children but also me. On the other hand, when I answer my kids harshly, it only serves to stir up their agitation and mine, thus prolonging the argument.

Is it difficult for you to respond to your family with a gentle answer? If so, you are not alone; however, there is help on the way! Ask God to help you respond differently today. He is faithful and He will do it. You can't do it on your own—it isn't what comes naturally. But with His intervention in your life, it can be done. He can help you have "a gentle answer."

Forgive me, Lord, when I major on the minors. Teach me how to respond with a gentle answer instead of a harsh reaction. Help me to pause before I respond so that you will have time to remind me how my words will sound to those I love. I love my family so much, but many times my tone of voice doesn't reflect that. Thank you for your Word, which has all the answers I need to be the best mom I can be. Amen.

MAMA**DRAMA**

Make it a practice as you spend time with God to ask Him what changes He wants from you, instead of always asking Him to change others around you. You might be surprised by what is revealed!

As moms, we have a tendency to immediately ask our children, "Why did you do such and such?" Most of the time they will not have an answer. Try taking the word "why" out of your vocabulary when correcting your children. That may help your responses become more "gentle."

Detour Ahead

W E WERE CLASHING about everything: clothes, hairstyles, careless actions, rolling eyes, and disrespectful remarks to my husband and me. Anything I said made her angry, and that made me furious! I was trying to think of something to say to her that would be considered "praise," but I wasn't coming up with much! How had we ended up here, on this bumpy detour? I didn't know. Panic set in as I wondered, "If she's like this at eight, what will the teen years hold for us?"

A couple of days into this relationship detour, we had dinner with some friends. After we left, their eighteen-year-old son commented to his mom, "There's just something special about her" (my daughter). The next day my friend called me and passed on the compliment. My mouth dropped open. "What?" I wanted to say. "Are we talking about the same demanding, argumentative kid?" The truth of Proverbs 15:23 was immediately revealed: "How good is a timely word."

For the rest of the day I looked at my daughter differently. I had been missing her. She wasn't the only one who was on this demanding and disagreeable detour! In fact, I think I had *driven* her there. (Pun completely intended!)

That little bit of praise from a trusted friend changed my perspective. Another friend told me at a particularly challenging time, "You know, maybe you're getting to deal with some of those attitudes *now* instead of during the teen years." I was filled with hope and strength to continue.

Those responses introduced me to a few things we need to remember. First, when I have a good word to pass on to another mom about her kids, I need to share it. Instead of noticing only the negative things, praising the good qualities I see in her child might rescue that mom from a deep struggle she is having with her child. Second, passing on a compliment gives that kid an important "I believe in you" message that they might desperately need to hear.

I shared with my daughter the encouraging comment that I

heard about her. When you hear those words as a kid, they have a way of sticking with you for the rest of your life. I know my daughter has that compliment filed away.

And one more thing: If you're on that disagreeable road with one of your kids, try to see it as a *detour*. Detours are time-consuming, confusing, and bumpy, but they eventually wind around and get back to the main road. Let God guide you so that you can guide your children.

I realized from the encouraging words of my friends that my daughter is amazing. You should meet her—there really is something special about her! Be encouraged. Your kids are amazing too!

> *Father, help me see when I have the opportunity to reach out and give encouragement to another mom. Remind me to tell my children about the compliments that others give me about them. And give me the endurance I need to see these detours for what they are—detours, not the finished road. Encourage me, Lord, with the words I need to hear about my children. I want to listen now for what you think of them.*
>
> (Write any thoughts you have about your children here:)

_____

_____

_____

_____

_____

_____

_____

_____

_____

> *Please fill me with hope, Lord. In Jesus' name, amen.*

MAMA**DRAMA**

Call a friend and share with her something you like about her child. If you can't think of anything, ask God to show you something.

Make a list of the things that you know are special about your child. Post it on your fridge for all (including your child) to see.

Reflecting Christ

"Mirror of Your Heart"

Her chubby hands, somehow they look like mine.
Those big blue eyes are like her dad's.
That pudgy nose, is it mine or his?
How can one person look like two?

This miracle sent from God above
She's so much more than I dreamed of.
She looks like us, does what we do.
Make our hearts look just like You.

A reflection of your heart
That's the most important part,
Not how they look or how tall they stand.
As they grow and learn each day
Guide them gently to your way
To be a mirror of your heart.

At night I hear his voice praying quietly
Trusting You with everything.
And through our day he reminds me of You
As he sweetly sings "Jesus loves me."

This miracle sent from God above
He's so much more than I dreamed of.
He's doing now just what You do.
His heart resembles You.

Family Resemblance

*I*SN'T IT FUNNY that as soon as a baby is born, everyone begins to suggest who the child resembles? I almost giggle out loud when I hear people say, "Oh, I think little Johnny looks like his daddy." The father of the child grins from ear to ear, taking the words spoken as a compliment. But three hours after his birth, can anyone really tell who this swollen, bloated, squished-faced baby is going to look like? Who in their right mind would want to admit to resembling their baby at this point?

It is true, however, that we like our kids to look like us. In fact, we are constantly looking for similarities that link them to us! The lyrics to the song say it well. "Her chubby hands, somehow they look like mine. Those big blue eyes are like her dad's. That pudgy nose, is it mine or his? How can one person look like two?"

After Addison was born, it was interesting to me that my older children were finding features in him that they thought resembled them. Abby said, "Mommy, he has my ears, doesn't he?" Avery chimed in, "And his mouth and nose look more like me and Alec, right?" We take pride in the thought that someone looks like us.

We know of a couple who adopted two children, a brother and sister. When I first saw the children I was amazed at how much they looked like their adoptive parents. It wasn't planned (except by God)—but of course the parents were thrilled by the resemblance.

Children may resemble not only their parents' physical features but also their mannerisms, attitudes, and personalities. Now *that's* a scary thought. The bad part is that we don't get to pick and choose *which* characteristics they will resemble.

We are children of God. And just as our children resemble us, we are to resemble our heavenly Father. So I have a question for you. When was the last time someone said, "You resemble someone . . . oh yeah, it's Jesus"? God adopted us and made us heirs to all He has and is. We are His children. John 1:12 says,

"Yet to all who received him, to those who believed in his name, he gave the right to become children of God."

Like us, God takes pride in looking at His kids and finding a family resemblance. I must admit that many times I look nothing like my heavenly Father. I long to resemble Him in my words and actions but fall short so often. I want to resemble Him not only for my own sake but also for the sake of my children, who are watching me. How will they ever resemble or reflect Him if they don't see me setting the example first?

I find comfort, however, in knowing that God's Spirit is at work all the time within me, transforming me into His image. Second Corinthians 3:18 says it well: "And we, who with unveiled faces all reflect the Lord's glory, are being transformed into his likeness with ever-increasing glory, which comes from the Lord, who is the Spirit."

Lord, I want my life to be a reflection of you, so that my children will be drawn to you. Thank you that you never give up on me. Continue to transform me into your likeness. Forgive me for the times when I've chosen to live like a prodigal, when I've gone my own way and ignored the fact that I was created in your image with a God-given "family resemblance." Thank you for adopting me into your family. Amen.

MAMA**DRAMA**

Write down what it means to you to "be a reflection of Christ." Look up the word *reflection* and meditate on how God wants to transform you into His likeness today. Sharon captured the thought well in the lyrics from "Mirror of Your Heart":

A reflection of your heart
That's the most important part,
Not how they look
Or how tall they stand.
As they grow and learn each day,
Guide them gently to your way
To be a mirror of your heart.

'Fess Up When You Mess Up!

L AST YEAR MY ten-year-old son, Alec, had a minor bicycle acci-
dent. He was headed to the Laundromat at an RV park to find
his dad so they could throw the football together. On the way, he
was trying to hold his football and steer his bike at the same
time. When his bicycle began to weave, Alec was thrust into the
small gutter on the side of the road. The jolt threw him off balance, and before he knew what was happening, he was falling side-
ways into the back of a Mercedes-Benz. (Why couldn't it have been
an old beat-up jalopy or something?) Anyway, his handlebar went
into the back of the taillight, leaving a teensy-tiny crack in it. It
was minuscule. It didn't chip the paint or leave even the smallest
dent. It was practically undetectable to the naked eye (especially
if you were several feet away).

Alec brushed himself off. He looked around, climbed back on
his bike, and headed out to find his dad. On the way he pondered
what he should do. *Should I tell Daddy? Or not? If I do tell, will he
get mad at me?* Poor kid, he probably wrestled a lot with what to
do, thinking, *No one saw what happened . . . and you can barely
even see the dent.*

Finally Alec made it to his destination. He did something that
day that I'm not sure many of us would have done. Our coura-
geous little boy had made his decision. He went inside, found his
dad, and told the truth, reluctantly stating, "Daddy, I hit a car."
To which his dad responded, "What kind was it?" (Is that a guy
response or what?)

Together, they walked to the car to inspect the damage. The
crack was small, but it was there. Charles explained that the owners might not see it, but the crack—even as small as it was—
would allow moisture to seep inside the light.

Charles left a note for the owners, saying they should call him
when they returned. It wasn't long until they called. Charles and
Alec went to 'fess up to the mess up! Charles suggested the owners get an estimate, and he'd pay for the repair.

Several weeks later we received a letter from the couple.

Enclosed was a straightforward note, saying something like, "The repairs for the taillight were $238.00. Thanks."

I'll bet you thought that they were going to reward Alec's honesty by not making him pay for the damages, didn't you? I have to say, I had also hoped there would be some kind of encouragement for his honesty. But it didn't happen. We had to pay the $238.00. Alec even paid fifty dollars of it out of his hard-earned money. (That's a lot for a ten-year-old!)

So does it pay to 'fess up when you mess up? Maybe not financially, but according to God's Word, it does pay. First John 1:9 says, "If we confess our sins, he is faithful and just and will forgive us our sins and purify us from all unrighteousness." There is no price tag that can be placed on the feeling of having a clean heart. It's something that money can't buy—the awesome reward promised by God when we are honest before Him.

Is it hard for you to 'fess up when you mess up? Is it difficult for you to admit when you're wrong? Is it tough for you to ask for forgiveness? Do you have a tendency to blame everyone else for your behavior? John 8:32 says, "Then you will know the truth, and the truth will set you free." There is freedom in truth. Your burden can be lifted and your tired heart strengthened by coming clean.

Lord God, you are Truth. I want to be drawn to your truth, not deceived by dishonesty. I long to experience the freedom that comes when I am honest before you and those I've hurt. Help me to be quick to acknowledge my wrongdoings, so I can be a good example for my children, showing them how to 'fess up when I mess up. Thank you for your patience with me. Amen.

MAMA**DRAMA**

If you are ever undercharged for an item (it could happen), use the opportunity to teach your children honesty. Go back and pay the difference.

When accidents happen, maybe the response should be, "I'm sorry." But when the offense is something you can control, the required response is, "Would you forgive me?"

A Cook in Training

MY SEVEN-YEAR-OLD daughter was helping me bake cookies (the frozen, break-apart kind . . . I hope that qualifies as "baking"). I asked her to spray the cookie sheet and, wow, did she spray it! She covered it completely, until there were little rivers of Pam running off the pan and onto the floor. It caught me off guard and I yelled, "Whoa! That's enough!" My sour face and harsh words were insensitive and condescending.

She looked at me with hurt in her eyes and said, "Oh, I'm sorry, Mommy. I was trying to get it on the edges." I was disgusted with myself. She loves to spend time with me, and what do I give her for making her best effort? The disapproving message, "You're doing it wrong! You should know better!" I apologized and told her, "It's okay, sweetie. You've never done it before. You can't learn until you have the chance to practice."

As a mom, it's easy for me to forget that my kids are kids and they *think* like kids. "When I was a child, I talked like a child, I thought like a child, I reasoned like a child" (1 Corinthians 13:11). To grow them past that childish thinking, I must train them. We train their minds and bodies in how to accomplish things: hanging up their clothes, doing their homework, using a mixer, hitting a baseball.

But we also train their hearts through our responses. This heart training is the hardest kind for me because so often the situations are unpredictable and can make my blood boil before I know it. It takes God's hand in my life to control my words when I can't control the situation.

Maybe you're feeling like a failure because you've responded harshly to your child's immaturity today. Ask them to forgive you, then ask God to help you respond in a loving "I accept you even if it doesn't work out" kind of way. Your acceptance of their small flops will help them persevere through the inevitable trials and failures they will face in life.

Lord, I feel so awful when I treat my children like they are a bother. I can see it in their eyes when they feel like they've disappointed me. It crushes me. I'm so grateful you have given me the responsibility of raising and training my children. Help me to encourage rather than discourage them. Forgive me for the times I've "blown it" with them.

As I go through my days, give me opportunities to train their minds, bodies, and hearts. Speak through me when my responses would normally be harsh and uncaring. I can't always see what's coming, Lord, but cover me with understanding and love. Help me enjoy where they are and enjoy that they do need me to teach them the simplest of things. Though it's sometimes stressful and scary, it is a privilege to shape the lives of my children. I need you. I can't do it on my own. Train me, Lord. In Jesus' name, amen.

MAMA**DRAMA**

If you have a chance to cook with your child today, prepare yourself beforehand by remembering that the kitchen will likely be a mess afterward; a little too much flour will go in the batter (and everywhere else), and they are going to want to eat more dough than you cook. How will you respond to those things? Sometimes thinking through a situation *before* it happens can make our responses softer and more understanding.

A great way to calm your nerves is to bake the cookies ahead of time, then let your kids help you ice them. Something that worked well for us was to buy clean paintbrushes, give the kids each a cup of frosting the thickness of paint, and let them paint their cookies.

Works-in-Progress

WE WERE WALKING through the mall and suddenly my daughter stumbled, then landed sprawled out across the floor. Before I checked to see if she was okay, I looked at her accusingly, as if she had done it on purpose, and said, "You need to slow down!"

Maybe she did need to slow down, but sometimes the embarrassment of falling can go further in helping her learn to slow down than my negative tone of voice or arched eyebrows. Experience can be the best teacher.

I am praying about this because, for me, to scold is my first thought. I know it is wrong to acknowledge their blunder without compassion. It's almost like the clumsiness is a reflection on me—that I haven't trained them to slow down or watch where they are going. A laugh at my child's expense isn't worth it either. God is working on me. I've heard that the first step to recovery is acknowledging you have a problem. Well, obviously I've got one!

In Matthew 7:1–2 (THE MESSAGE) it says, "Don't pick on people, jump on their failures, criticize their faults—unless, of course, you want the same treatment. That critical spirit has a way of boomeranging." Ouch! It's true! I've noticed my kids following in my footsteps at times, laughing instead of responding with compassion.

Sometimes I say what I'm thinking too soon. Ephesians 4:29 is a good reminder. "Do not let any unwholesome talk come out of your mouths, but only what is *helpful for building others up* according to their needs, that it may *benefit those who listen.*" When you and I have the opportunity to say anything about our children in public, what we say will either benefit them or tear them down.

Gretchen, a friend of ours with nine children, shared some of the comments she hears when she and the kids (all under the age of twelve) go to the grocery store. "Are they all yours? I'm so sorry." To which she thinks, *Sorry for what?* Sometimes they say, "Don't you know what causes that?" and she thinks, *Yes, and we like it!*

She said, "Every chance I get, I tell complete strangers how great my kids are. They are well-mannered, happy, responsible, God-focused *works-in-progress.* I want my children to hear that I am so thrilled they are mine, that God could give no greater riches to me than my children."

I forget that sometimes. Our children are works-in-progress. If you've forgotten, like me, and have messed up, remember: Today is a new day. If your morning was bad, get a fresh start this afternoon. If the last hour was bad, this is a new moment. Apologize if you need to, then ask God to help you show your "works-in-progress" that they are your greatest treasures.

Ask God to help you remember that they are growing (and aren't comfortable with the size of their feet yet), so you can show compassion and use encouraging words instead of "kicking them when they're down." We have the opportunity to benefit those who are listening to us!

You may struggle as I do, forgetting to kiss the hurt before asking "why" or wipe the tears before a frown covers my face. Write your own prayer to God today, praying that He will spark concern before a compassionless response jumps out of your mouth. He is able!

Dear Lord, you know the effect of my words . . .

_____

_____

_____

_____

. . . Knowing you are able to change my most engrained responses, I ask all of this in Jesus' name, amen.

MAMA**DRAMA**

If you have poked fun at your child, especially in public, ask your child to forgive you. You might even need to ask those who were with you to forgive you too.

Fill a "treasure box" with jewels or pretty flowers and use it as a centerpiece. Tell your family that God could not have given you any treasure greater than them. Write and include in the treasure box the verse quoted earlier from Ephesians 4:29. Our words can be treasures for those we love. (Wooden boxes and jewels are available at craft stores. Be sure to paint your treasure box gold!)

Divine Appointments

THE INDIANA STATE Fairgrounds is not a very likely place to meet God. But God doesn't always come in familiar sanctuaries. He likes to surprise us with gentle reminders.

As my sister and I were homeschooling our children on the lawn of the fairgrounds, we were approached by someone who looked like a policeman. He asked if our children would like to pick some flowers. Having told our children hundreds of times not to pick the flowers, what a delight it was to let them! We followed the kind gentleman to the flower bed where about fifteen women, prisoners from a local facility, were cleaning out the weeds and post-season flowers.

The kids immediately befriended these precious ladies as they filled bags with their picked flowers. The ladies' eyes sparkled as they watched the kids. After a while the little girls were sitting in their laps and decorating the prisoners' hair with flowers! They talked with these ladies like they had known them for years.

For the women who had children of their own and were missing them, the unexpected visit by our little angels stirred up in them both a thankfulness and a sadness. With tears in her eyes, one mom shared about the two children she so desperately missed.

We left that day blessed beyond belief. I was struck by both the women and the prison guard we had met. The women were not what I had always envisioned "prisoners" to be. They weren't hard, tough, or unkempt ladies. They were beautiful. I realized how quick I am to judge before I know the true situation!

And the prison guard wasn't what I always imagined a prison guard to be either. His gentleness and genuine admiration for these ladies was obvious. He treated them with the utmost respect and believed each one of them would be an asset to society again.

Our two families are in "full-time ministry." At least, that's our occupation. There are days that full time, in my mind, can only refer to the minutes we are "onstage" or the time we are preparing to be "onstage" before a group of moms. But this gentleman reminded me that the call on all of our lives, no matter what our occupation may be, is to be in full-time ministry—to our families and those we happen to meet.

Knowing God can make changes we can't imagine, we can encourage others, believing in them when the world doesn't. We can take time for people, no matter who or where they are. That's what Jesus did. That's why Jesus died. That day at the Indiana State Fairgrounds, God reminded me that just because people mess up doesn't mean He is finished with them—He might just be getting started!

Several weeks after our surprise visit with these ladies, we were excited to receive this email from one of the inmates:

> Dear Laurie & Sharon,
>
> You may not remember me, but I met you and your children at the Indiana State Fairgrounds. At the time I was an inmate at the Correctional Facility. Just to refresh your memory, we picked flowers with your children. The reason I am writing to you is to thank you. You have no idea how much that day meant to all of us! I was released and now am in the process of reestablishing myself in society, but mainly with my two children, a boy who is eight, and my five-year-old daughter. They are the light in my life, and spending those few precious moments with you two wonderful ladies and your beautiful children was a gift from God. And I thank Him every day for bringing us together on that day. Most of the ladies that were with me on that road crew are still incarcerated. And I still communicate with a couple of them. I told them that I would write to you and thank you for allowing us a few minutes of freedom, where there was none for us. So thank you from the bottom of our hearts. I pray that God is with you and your family, in all that you do.
>
> May God Bless You.

Oh, the joy we would have missed had we shunned these ladies that day. I'm thankful God helped us see beyond the blue shirts and the gun worn by the prison guard. God has plans for all of us, not just people in full-time ministry. God's plan for us is to love those we meet and those we live with each day. That's pretty much full-time ministry, don't you think?

I wonder what divine engagement God has in store for you today. As you serve your family, go through the grocery store, or go to work, keep your eyes open for these moments orchestrated by the Lord. They aren't accidents. They are divine appointments.

Lord, what a compassionate God you are! I want to be more like you. I pray that you'll help me see past the outward appearance of people that I meet today . . . even if I only come in contact with the people in my home. Use me, Lord. Fill me with your thoughts so that my life will reflect your acceptance and love. You are the God of many chances. I pray that I'll be willing to give others, including my family, a second, third, fourth, or thirtieth chance. Thank you, Lord, for never giving up on us. I love you! In Jesus' name I pray, amen.

MAMA**DRAMA**

Ask God as you go through your day to show you where He is working. Slow down so you won't miss those divine appointments at the grocery store, a child's ball practice, in phone conversations, or at dinner with your family.

Learning to Lean

"Oil and perfume make the heart glad,
So a man's counsel is sweet to his friend."

Proverbs 27:9 (NASB)

A Little to the Left

A LITTLE TO THE left, down a little, no, up, over.... Aaahhh, right there. Doesn't it feel better when someone else scratches your back? If you have that one spot that is really bugging you, the one you can't reach, it's hard to make it feel better without a friend! Struggles in life can be the same way.

For some reason, in our culture we have been fed the message that we should be able to handle it all. We have taken that information as the truth and can drive ourselves (and our families) crazy trying to live up to it. It's not that we don't have friends, but they are often just surface friends because we're trying to keep the appearance that things are fine.

One mom wrote, "I wish more moms would be honest. We would learn so much from each other if we were. When my daughter was a baby, I could have used another mom telling me that she didn't always feel happy either. Instead, I received the opposite. So I thought something was wrong with me.

"I discovered later that my friends were experiencing the same trials, but they wouldn't talk about it. Now I share as much as I can about my kiddos, school, home, life, or whatever. I am discovering that other moms will share similar experiences if I do, allowing us both to breathe a big sigh of relief! I always tell my friends that my children aren't perfect, and our lives would be so boring if they were! Even though there are days when boring would be nice, we wouldn't have it any other way!"

What feels better: Holding in the frustrations while trying to keep it together, or letting people in on what's difficult for you? There are lots of annoying "itches" in our lives—a rebellious child, an in-law relationship gone bad, a struggle with weight, financial hardships, feelings of inadequacy as a mom. When we won't get deep with each other it's like having a spot that needs to be scratched, but there are no friendly fingernails to help out!

So let other people in on your life, sharing not just the happenings of your days but the mishaps as well. The Bible says, "Two are better than one.... If one falls down, his friend can help him up" (Ecclesiastes 4:9–10).

Just as we can't scratch every spot on our backs, so we shouldn't expect to handle life on our own either. When we decide to dive in and share with someone, we have the chance to learn from them and have our burden lightened a little.

If you only have "surface" friends, ask God to show you how to grow deeper with them or give you other friends who can walk alongside you in life. We all need a scratch now and then.

> *Lord, as women, we try to handle many things at the same time. It's easy for us to feel like we have failed if we can't balance it all. Even in that struggle, we often try to keep a smile on our faces. I pray you'll help us realize that it's hard for all of us. None of us has it together. I pray for the mom who is reading this and feels so defeated. Help her, Lord, to cling tightly to you. Give her a friend, maybe a friend who is going through this devotional book, to share her struggle. If she has just moved and hasn't found friends, I pray that you would put someone in her path to help her get connected.*
>
> *Give all of us the courage to share with each other. We feel like we're losing it sometimes, God. Strengthen us. Help us turn to you. Help us to begin chipping away at the wall that has kept us from sharing our hard times. You are a good God. Thank you for loving us and being our constant Friend. In Jesus' name I pray, amen.*

MAMA**DRAMA**

A pastor once shared, "Why is it that we only hear about the struggles people have been through? Why can't we go through it with them?" What are you going through right now that you would like to share with someone? Write it down and then ask God for the opportunity to share it with an understanding friend.

Quarantined, but Not Contagious

AFTER HAVING MY first child, I found myself lonely, isolated, and cut off from the rest of the world. Because I had worked full time prior to becoming a stay-at-home mom, I had been constantly surrounded by co-workers, people who offered support and encouragement.

Now the only support I felt I had was from the underwire nursing bra that was holding up the two rocks on my chest. I felt as if I had been quarantined to my home. I felt trapped amid unending messes and taunted by unfinished tasks.

It caught me by surprise, this feeling of loneliness, because motherhood was something I had longed for. I couldn't complain. After all, this was what I had *chosen.* So why was I feeling so miserable? Why didn't someone tell me how hard this transition was going to be? It was remarkably harder than I had ever imagined.

Fearful that someone might see that I was really struggling in my new role, I made sure that I always put on a "happy face." I acted as if things were great, but the whole time I was longing for someone who could understand, someone who had been there, someone who would listen. It wasn't until Sharon and I began speaking to moms that I realized how many moms struggle with loneliness. I was not the only mom who had experienced such feelings. They too had experienced the same isolation in their lives.

What a waste, I thought. If only I had risked being more vulnerable with other moms when my kids were little, I could have found support. If only I had been willing to take a chance, go out on a limb, put my insecurities out there . . . not only could I have been relieved of the burdens I was bearing all alone, but I also could have lightened the load of loneliness for someone else.

We have the crazy idea that we should have it all together, that we have to daily be confident and content in the role of motherhood. We believe that since it was our choice to be a mom, we shouldn't struggle with negative emotions. The truth, however, is that *all moms experience such feelings* at one time or another. There is no need to suffer by holding it all in. We would be much better moms if we would share the feelings that seem to entrap us.

During those days when I was so lonely, I would have been so much better if only I'd heeded 1 Thessalonians 5:11, which says, "Therefore encourage one another and build each other up, just as in fact you are doing." We need each other. We are not meant to go it alone. Someone needs you as much as you need them. Encourage one another today.

> *Father, even when I feel so alone, I'm really not. You are always with me. As I adjust to the role I'm in, help me to be a little more honest with others about how I'm feeling. Lord, forgive me when pride keeps me from being an encouragement to others because I don't want to let anyone in. Put someone in my path who needs encouragement today. In your name, amen.*

MAMA**DRAMA**

The next time you are out in public with your kids—at Wal-Mart, McDonald's, baseball practice, etc.—be transparent as you talk with other moms. You will be surprised to discover that you are not alone after all!

If you are transitioning from a work environment to being a stay-at-home mom, give it time. For many moms it might take one or two years to settle into this new career. I've been there. It is a *huge* change. Don't give up too soon!

Wide-Eyed Conversational Prayers

THE SUMMER BEFORE we were married, my husband-to-be and I drove from Texas to Florida for a reunion with some of his family and friends. On our way back, before we arrived at his parents' house, he said, "Have you ever prayed conversational prayers?"

"What does that mean?" I asked.

"Well, I'll pray a sentence or two about what is on my heart, then you can pray whatever God puts on your heart, then I'll pray again, and you can pray again if you want."

I was confused. "But, sweetie, we're driving. How are you going to bow your head and close your eyes?" (That's the way we normally prayed!)

He laughed and said, "You don't have to close your eyes to pray."

I knew that. I had prayed with my eyes open before a test or when I was in a conversation with someone and I didn't really know how to answer. I would ask God to give me the words I needed. The difference was, I was praying by myself, in my head.

But praying aloud, with my eyes open, with someone else, was weird for me. I had also prayed in a circle where one would pray, then squeeze your hand when they were done. But this was different; it was random. There were no assigned turns.

I told him I would give it a try. I followed his lead as he began talking to God with his eyes open while we were driving. It was awkward at first, but then I was thrilled with the freedom I had to pray for things that God put on my heart, even things that I was seeing as we drove down the highway.

We thanked God for the amazing trees in Mississippi and the beautiful Kudzu "monsters." I prayed for the drivers that we passed—for their safety and that Jesus would open their eyes to see their need for Him if they hadn't realized it yet. I let my eyes look deeper and deeper into the sky and thanked God for His majesty. The prayer bounced back and forth between us as we agreed together over the things we were speaking. We prayed about our upcoming marriage and our future children. The result? I was closer to the Lord and closer to this man I would soon call my husband.

Now, after twelve years of marriage, we are both much more comfortable with talking to God *together*. The thing I love about conversational prayer is that I don't have to think of everything I want to pray in one long prayer. The Holy Spirit can use something Pat says to prompt a thought in me.

The Bible says, "When two of you get together on anything at all on earth and make a prayer of it, my Father in heaven goes into action. And when two or three of you are together because of me, you can be sure that I'll be there" (Matthew 18:19–20 THE MESSAGE).

I am amazed that God loves us enough to listen to us and to be there with us. He is never absent! Wow! The power of heaven is moved into action when we pray, and especially when we pray together. So try it with your family or a friend. Join me now as we praise Him through prayer . . . together!

Lord, You are amazing, _____

_____

_____. *Thank you for giving us the*

ability to talk with you, the creator of all the earth. _____

_____

_____

_____. *We praise you for*

the gifts you have given us, gifts like your Word, _____

_____, *your gift of love,*

_____, *hope,*

_____

a fresh start every day, _____

_____, *sleep for our weary bodies and minds,*

_____,

_____. *Help*

us to listen to you, _____

_____. *We want to learn from you,* _____

_____. *Remind us to talk*

to you all through our day, _____

_____. *Thank you for bringing good out*

of all things. _____.

We know it's because of Jesus that we can come to you like this, so in His name we pray, amen and amen.

MAMA**DRAMA**

Try conversational prayer with your kids. If you're in the car, just pray as you're driving along seeing God's creation. Or try it at bedtime—it's less distracting if you turn out the lights. We've prayed this way a few times with our kids. We just have a hard time getting our three-year-old to understand "short"!

Looking Forward

L AURIE AND I had the privilege of spending time with some childhood friends who were ahead of us in the parenting process. The conversation grew from casual catching up ("How old are your kids now?") to the deeper issues we were all facing. We listened as one mom told us with tears in her eyes how she missed her daughter. Although the daughter hadn't moved out of the house yet, the mom explained, "When she turned sixteen her time with us was replaced with a driver's license, a job, and a boyfriend. I hardly see her. She calls me on her cell phone, but it sometimes feels awkward and a little strained because we no longer have much in common. We don't have much to discuss.

Other moms agreed that this time had sort of taken them by surprise. They hadn't seen it coming. I always thought that we had our kids until they were eighteen years old. Now I was hearing that my main "mom time" with them was being cut short by two years. Not that we won't still have an impact on their lives, but from what I was hearing, it was less about training and more about learning to let go during those years. I was thankful to know about that two-year loss *now*, instead of being surprised by it in a few years.

Not long after that conversation, our daughter celebrated her ninth birthday. My husband commented, "We're halfway there with her, honey." I thought about it, then said, "We're more than halfway there." I wanted to cry. Where had the time gone? The conversation with my friends had given me the chance to realize time was passing. It put a fire in me, an urgency to pour into my daughter all that we feel God wants us to give her while we still have time.

After that weekend Laurie and I both realized the value of having friends ahead of us who could give us wisdom and advice about what is to come. Having others who have been there helps you prepare for the changes, rather than be shocked by them. Not that the different stages will be easy, but knowing they are coming can eliminate the surprise. "The right word spoken at the right time is as beautiful as gold apples in a silver bowl" (Proverbs 25:11 NCV).

Often we only have friends who are at the same stage as we are—with children the same age as ours. There are good reasons for this. Schedules are very different for moms with older kids, and little kids play well with other little kids.

Yet there is value in having access to the wisdom of more seasoned moms. If you've found yourself with no "older mom" friends, ask God to bring them into your life—moms who will encourage you to cherish what you have and share the right words at the right time about what might be coming in the future. There is much to be discovered from those who have walked the road a few years before. Listen to them. Let them share. Learn from them. They are a gift.

Lord, you know all the plans for us and our children, as well as the stages and changes that are ahead. Thank you for moms who have experienced more of life with kids, who can encourage us to enjoy where we are and give insight on where we are going. I pray you will let our paths cross with moms like that. Thank you for your gifts of friendship. In Jesus' name, amen.

MAMA**DRAMA**

You might try to connect over lunch with a friend who has older kids. These two questions are good conversation starters to move from general topics to deeper issues: "What are some things you did right with your kids?" And, "If you had it to do all over again, what would you do differently?"

Tell Him About It

AT CHRISTMAS one year Britt told me, "Oh, Momma, I want to tell you something Daddy got you for Christmas soooo bad!" With that she slapped her hand over her mouth, then uncovered it to say, "I have to get it out!" She tucked her head under my bed, muttered it into her hand, and came out with a deep sigh and a big smile.

Have you ever had a piece of information that you were just dying to tell? Something that was burning within you? You may even think, *If I share this, other people will know to pray, so it's okay to share it.* Maybe it's something you heard secondhand. You know you shouldn't pass it on, but instead of slapping your hand over your mouth, you allow it to fly out. Gossip is an addicting habit, isn't it?

"I find it is impossible to pray for and gossip about a person at the same time. I can't thank God for all the good things about a person and be filled with accusations at the same time."[1] What a great cure for the urge to spread rumors: pray for the person! Proverbs 26:20 says, "Without wood a fire goes out; without gossip a quarrel dies down."

If there is something going on in your church or community, do your part to make the gossiping end. Stop talking about it. You can pray for all involved, but don't talk about it. Paul gives excellent advice in the following Scripture: "Though some tongues just love the taste of gossip, Christians have better uses for language than that. Don't talk dirty or silly. That kind of talk doesn't fit our style. Thanksgiving is our dialect" (Ephesians 5:3-4 THE MESSAGE).

So how can we stop ourselves from gossiping? You might not stick your head under the bed like my daughter, but what about using your closet to mutter your news to God? Get it out by telling Him about it. Then come out of the closet, breath a sigh of relief, smile, and move on.

Lord, you know our hearts. You say that "out of the over-flow of the heart, the mouth speaks. The good man brings good things out of the good stored up in him, and the evil man brings evil things out of the evil stored up in him" (Matthew 12:34–35).

Show us where the evil is coming from, and help us have the courage to stop putting evil into our hearts. Remind us to pray instead of speaking words that should never be uttered. "May the words of my mouth and the meditation of my heart be pleasing in your sight, O Lord, my Rock and my Redeemer" (Psalm 19:14). *In Jesus' name I pray, amen.*

MAMA**DRAMA**

Work on memorizing Proverbs 26:20: "Without wood a fire goes out; without gossip a quarrel dies down," or one of the other verses mentioned. When you put His Word in your heart, He can use it to jog your memory when you need the reminder.

Mouth Monitor Needed

"Set a guard over my mouth, O Lord;
keep watch over the door of my lips."

Psalm 141:3

A Few Words to the Public

$\mathcal{I}$ SAT WAITING as my tires were being rotated, when a grand-father walked in with his adorable little grandson who looked to be about four years old. With his buzz haircut and big eyes, the little boy was practically irresistible. The owner of the tire shop noticed the little guy too and said, "That's a good-looking boy you've got there." I listened for the grandpa's response. My wide-eyed smile fell when he sarcastically commented, "Oh, he's trouble!"

How do you respond to that? The owner ran his hand over the little fella's stubby hair in comfort. My heart hurt for the boy. I thought about the great opportunity that this grandfather had been given to publicly build this little boy up, and he missed it.

Have you done that? I have. It's easy to do. Sometimes we're so frustrated with our kids that when someone says they are well behaved, we want them to know the truth: "You should see them at home!" Or if someone says, "They look like so much fun," it's tempting to reply, "You wanna take 'em home with you?"

A mom shared with us that when answering the phone, her husband always greets the caller with, "Trevor and Parker's proud father." Isn't that great? That dad is taking every opportunity to build his little guys up "in public" where his kids can hear. I'm sure they'll always remember that! Fred Hartley, Jr., author of *Parenting at Its Best,* said, "The only thing better than *personally* receiving a sincere compliment is *publicly* receiving a sincere compliment." [1]

One grandma told us, "What you say about your child in front of someone else is what they'll remember." Laurie and I, along with our brother, know that she's right. We remember our dad introducing each of us to strangers as his "right-hand man."

We didn't mind him calling us that. I was so excited that he was glad to be with me that I cherished the title of "right-hand *man.*" After his words of public praise, I wholeheartedly helped him in any way I could.

God modeled this public approval for His son as well. After

Jesus was baptized, "A voice from heaven said, 'This is my Son, whom I love; with him I am well pleased' " (Matthew 3:17). Jesus had the blessing of His father, complete with a public declaration of approval.

Our kids need that approval from us too. The next time you have the chance to publicly compliment your kids, don't miss it! What you say about your kids in front of someone is what they'll remember.

> *O Lord, our mouths are so hard to control. But you can use them for encouraging those we love. We know what it feels like to be embarrassed in public. Help us not be guilty any longer of putting our children (or husbands) through that humiliation. Please help us to pause and consider before we spout off what we're thinking. Help us care more about our children than the stranger we've just met and might never see again.*
>
> *Forgive us, Lord, for the times we belittle our children. I know it grieves your heart. Grow us. Teach us. Guide our words that they may encourage the little ears around us. In Jesus' name we pray, amen.*

MAMA**DRAMA**

Right now, think of a positive way to introduce your child so the next time you are given the opportunity you'll be ready! What are they good at? Maybe you could comment, "This is my singer," or "She is so generous," or "He (or she!) is my right-hand man!" Feel free to use my daddy's line—he won't mind a bit!

What would you have wanted your parents to say when someone commented on your good behavior or kind actions? Determine now to simply say "thank you" when you next hear a sweet comment about your child, rather than, "You should see them at home," or "You wanna take them home with you?"

Mouth Traps

I SUFFER FROM a disorder that I call STMI (Spouting Too Much Information). In other words, sometimes I say too much! For moms who are tired, irritable, and weary, it is very difficult not to say everything we are thinking. Consider this verse from the Bible: "By our speech we can ruin the world, turn harmony to chaos, throw mud on a reputation, send the whole world up in smoke and go up in smoke with it" (James 3:6 THE MESSAGE). Wow, that's pretty scary!

So how is it that we can use words so loosely? Why is taking control of our mouths so hard? God's Word tells it like it is in James 3:8: "No man can tame the tongue. It is a restless evil, full of deadly poison." Wow, that's harsh; but unfortunately it's the truth.

Even though I'm aware that my words can tear down another person, I can't seem to gain control of my tongue. Many times an ugly word slips out of my mouth before I sift it through the "good or ugly" filter; I just hate that! And being women (who like to talk a lot), we have numerous opportunities to offend others. (Isn't that an encouraging thought?)

For example, an easy "mouth trap" for me to fall into is sharing my frustrations about my husband in front of others. I *know* my friends can all relate. And of course they will be on *my* side. When women get together, we are easily tempted to enter into a husband-bashing session. Maybe you've joined in discussions like these:

"Does your husband put his dirty clothes in the hamper or just drop them on the floor?" "I've asked my husband to hang a picture on the wall fifty-five times, and it's still sitting on top of the dresser." "My husband is totally oblivious to the needs of the children. I have to do everything." "My husband just won't talk to me." "He doesn't even recognize or appreciate *all* I do for our family."

Today I realized that I'd said too much—again. Not only had I talked about my husband in front of some friends, I had also done it in front of my children. I was grumbling about my husband just yesterday, as I picked up his clothes off the floor again, and realized too late that my son was standing nearby. He quickly joined in my grumbling and stated, "Daddy *always* leaves his clothes out." I tried to act as if I was kidding, but the damage had already been done. Children are like sponges, soaking up every word we say as quickly as it is spoken.

See how we are? We just spur one another on! When we cut down, complain, or grumble about our husband, or anyone else for that matter, it only serves to magnify the problem and justify our discontent. It also serves to produce negative thoughts in those who listen.

Does it make us feel better when we spout off about others? Maybe it helps temporarily, but most of the time it is a mouth trap, one that leaves our witness lifeless in its grasp. I might try to justify my unkind words, but the reality is *it is sin.*

You might be thinking, *I have to vent to someone or I'll go crazy.* I have been there, and I know what you mean. There are definitely times in our lives when we need to share our burdens with another loyal friend, one who can provide godly counsel and direction. But when we have the wrong attitude and are simply seeking to find support for our feelings of resentment and discontent, then it becomes a sin.

Where are you today? How have you used your words lately . . . to tear down or build up? Be careful. Don't get caught in a mouth trap—they can be deadly!

Lord, I know that my words are powerful tools. Help me to use my words to help, not harm. "Set a guard over my mouth, O Lord; keep watch over the door of my lips" (Psalm 141:3). Help me remember that the words I speak influence the hearts of those listening. Lord, guard my words, that I might avoid the mouth traps that can so easily entangle me and hurt others. In Jesus' name I pray, amen.

MAMA**DRAMA**

What do your children hear you say about their dad? (It doesn't matter whether you are divorced or not.) As difficult as it might be, don't bash your spouse or ex-spouse. Our children's views are greatly influenced by our words.

Today, try bragging on your husband in front of your children.

Words of Hope

SEVERAL YEARS ago, at bedtime, I would tell my daughter, "I'm so excited about all God has planned for your life." She never had anything to say about my comment, so I didn't think she was listening. One day after I had complimented her about cleaning up all on her own (an unusual thing for her to do), she replied, "I bet God has all kinds of things planned for me!" She was hopeful about her future.

Now that my daughter is a little older, and we have added more children, I haven't been pouring that hope for the future into her like I did when she was a preschooler. I've noticed that she hasn't been as confident about those plans God has for her. She is often self-conscious, second-guesses herself, and worries that she has done something wrong. A common phrase right now is, "Mommy, would you forgive me for all the things I've done today?" I had forgotten the impact that my words (or lack of them) can have.

Proverbs 18:21 says, "The tongue has the power of life and death." Like a compass, we are able to set the course for our children, pointing them in the way they should go. Our words are a powerful tool in leading them. "Communicating a special future to a child is such an important part of giving a blessing. When a person feels in his or her heart that the future is hopeful and something to look forward to, it can greatly affect his or her attitude on life." [2]

One of our friends shared that every night she told her kids, "Out of all the kids in the whole world, I would still choose you." And even though her son is now seventeen, she still says to him, "I know you've heard it over and over, but out of all the kids . . ." They never get too old to hear that we're proud of them.

As we are the compass for our children, God wants to be our compass, guiding us into the words and ways that can give our children hope for the future. The truth is, with the Lord, the future is bright for our children and for us. Even through tough circumstances, there is hope when we are walking with Him.

Lord, life happens so fast sometimes that I don't feel like I consider what I'm going to say before I say it. Words just come out before I think. Fill my heart and mind with words that will encourage and uplift, words that will give my children life and hope knowing that they are part of your plan. Help me to not miss the opportunities that you give every day to point their hearts toward their future with you. Thank you, Holy Spirit, for being my compass, gently leading me. Lead on . . . in Jesus' name I pray, amen.

MAMADRAMA

If you don't already have a compass in your car, find one to hang over your rear-view mirror. When you see it, be reminded that God is your compass and you are the navigator of your children's hearts.

Here are some other great things to say to your kids:

"You will be a good friend to people all through your life."

"You really have a way of making people feel comfortable. God could use that to help people stay calm in a troubling time."

"You are so creative. I wonder how God will use that gift as you grow older."

"God has great plans for your life—not just later on, but right now too. I'm glad I get to watch you grow up!"

"You really do have big muscles! I think God gave you those so you could help people and protect your sisters."

From the Basement
to the Balcony

ONE DAY MY daughter told her aunt to "shut up." We don't say that in our family, and she knew it. Pat asked her where she had heard that expression, and she replied, "Dinina" (our next-to-perfect baby-sitter). When she saw her daddy wasn't buying her answer, she quickly changed her story to, "Satan . . . yeah, Satan."

I'm with her! There are some moments that I try to be nice, but it doesn't work. So instead of taking the blame, I'd rather place the responsibility on someone else. I'm in the basement, and I want to drag anyone else I can down with me! It's a gloomy and sometimes scary place to be. As a mom, it's easy for me to get stuck down below.

My words and actions are dark, sad, and probably, at times, scary to my children (and hubby too!). Basement days are those days that I can't recall saying "yes" to anything my children asked—days that I say "don't" fifty bazillion times, and I catch a glimpse of myself in the mirror and wonder how the wicked witch could have snuck into our house without my knowing it!

As moms, it's easy for us to be basement people. Part of the reason is that there is so much correction, protection, and civility to pass on to our children. We can get in a rut of negative correction rather than training them in a loving way. First Peter 5:2–3 says, "Care for God's flock with all the diligence of a shepherd. Not because you have to, but because you want to please God. Not calculating what you can get out of it, but acting spontaneously. *Not bossily telling others what to do, but tenderly showing them the way*" (THE MESSAGE, emphasis added).

We've all been around people that are basement influences in our lives. They drag us down and make us feel perfectly awful! On the other hand, a balcony person can encourage us like no other. They believe in us and don't mind saying so. We leave a conversation with them feeling like we could run a marathon! The good news is: We can be that balcony person for our children. They need us to come up from the basement, shine light, and breathe fresh air into their insecure, changing lives.

What kind of mom have you been lately? What about today? As we said before, just because you might have had a basement morning doesn't mean you have to have a complete basement day. Ask your children and God to forgive you, then talk to God about helping you see the positive things in your family.

Ask Him to give you creative ways to correct. Ask Him to lead you as you seek to "tenderly show them the way." And seek His help in not freaking out about things like spills, stains, running in the house, or preschoolers who are determined not to take naps. Ask Him to help you lighten up and have fun with your kids.

Sometimes we nail our shoes to the floor of the basement because we aren't willing to budge on anything. Every chance you have, laugh *with* your kids. Stop and play. Just do it! Let them flick water in your face and squeal. Get on the floor and flip them or wrestle. Let them help with lunch, and count on having mustard stain their clothes or pickles fall on the floor.

Your child is more valuable to you than any "thing" could ever be. When you slip back into the basement ruts, remind yourself that you don't have to stay there. It's just a few short steps to the balcony!

Lord, it is easy for me to get stuck in the basement. Forgive me. Help me to forgive myself. I need your strength to be a balcony mom. Help me to correct without demeaning my child. Help me to remember I'm training, not fixing. And remind me that my child and I are different. What is important to me isn't always going to be the top priority on their list. Move me out of my deep ruts of habit. Give me the energy, I pray, to be a balcony mom. Thanks for being a balcony, God, to me. . . . In Jesus' name, amen.

MAMA**DRAMA**

Stop and play today. Get into their world and laugh with them. Shoot hoops, play the animal game (acting like you're a kitty cat, horse, jaguar, elephant, or mouse), play dress-up, paint, let them fix your hair, play hide-and-seek. Slow down and have fun.

A Goose With News

WE WERE AT Yellowstone National Park, and I had slipped away early one morning to spend time with God and enjoy His creation. Even though I was cautiously watching for buffalo, it was actually a goose that distracted me.

Have you ever heard a goose honk? Talk about distracting! This one lone goose was flying overhead. I guess I had always heard geese honking together, but then it didn't sound so funny. Yet this one goose, all by herself, now had me laughing out loud. She sounded so silly! She kept on honking, despite my laughing. I heard her in the distance still honking. By this time, I was a little annoyed with her. She had something to say and she was determined to tell everybody at Yellowstone!

Her persistence reminded me of women and their news. I'm guilty of flying and honking what I know to anybody and everybody, but who is it really helping?

At my first job, right out of high school, people would always have "news" about a co-worker that they wanted to share with me. I don't know why I did this, but I would always stop them and say, "I think good of that person. Is what you're telling me going to make me think better of them?" That usually stopped the honking! "Listening to gossip is like eating cheap candy; do you really want junk like that in your belly?" (Proverbs 18:8 THE MESSAGE).

As a teacher, I remember how difficult it was to duck gossip about students or a fellow teacher. Sometimes it was presented as, "Out of *concern,* I want to tell you about this child." After hearing something negative about a person, the tendency is to start expecting those things from the person.

I wasn't just hearing the gossip, though. I remember going back to my room one day after just telling another teacher about the ins and outs of this one kid. I sat down at my desk and thought, *What have I done?* I had just given her information that made her think badly of a child she had really enjoyed. Would she now find it easier to jump to conclusions about him, rather than giving him the benefit of the doubt?

Proverbs 13:17 (THE MESSAGE) says, "Irresponsible talk makes a real mess of things."

Are you like the goose with news? Before we start honking our news or listening to someone else's gossip, maybe we could ask ourselves this question: "Is this going to make us think better of the person?" If not, don't honk about it. It becomes annoying after a while.

What have you said about someone else lately? Use this prayer time to confess anything you need to. When we gossip, we don't just offend people; God is offended as well. I'm so glad that He is a forgiving God!

_____

_____

_____

_____

MAMA**DRAMA**

Now that you've confessed to God, do you need to make things right with someone you have hurt by gossiping? Even if it means calling a friend from elementary school, middle school, or high school to ask their forgiveness, do it. If you know their current last name and city, you can look them up on *www.whitepages.com*. You can't take away the hurt, but you can ease it as you mend the relationship.

The Honorable Role of Serving

"Whatever I Do"

I clean the tub and scrub the floor and drive the kids to school.
Wash a dish and give a hug and preach the Golden Rule.
I look around, so much to do, when will it ever end?
But whether in my words or deeds, I'll do it for You.

Whatever I do I'll do it for You.
No matter how small, Lord, You see them all.
To be faithful in the little things is all You ask of me.
Whatever I do I'll do it for You.

Sometimes I feel the things I do are meaningless
and trite.
They don't amount to very much in other people's eyes.
But a job well done is not determined by its size.
But whether in my words or deeds, I'll do it for You.

It doesn't matter whether I become a gourmet chef
or make it to the top, climb that ladder of success.
It doesn't matter if I ever speak to crowds with ease.
Whether in my words or deeds, I'll do it for You.

Faithfulness is all You ask of me.

Words by Laurie Hilliard
Music by Laurie Hilliard and Joe Hargrave
Based on Colossians 3:23–24

Dairy Queen

SHARON AND I were at a convention recently. We stopped at one of the exhibit booths that featured fun "girlie" items, when my eyes were drawn to the adorable door charms. I immediately focused in on the one stating, *The Queen Is Sleeping.* I looked at Sharon and laughed, "I can't relate to any part of that. Can you? I don't feel like a queen, and I'm not getting much sleep these days!" Addison, my four-month-old, makes sure of that!

As I pondered the idea of being the "Queen" of my home, I began to have my own little pity party. I pouted, thinking, *I feel more like the maidservant than a queen. . . . No one ever serves me. I'm the one who does all the serving. And by the way, shouldn't the queen be adored by her husband? . . . I don't think my husband knows what that word means.*

Several days passed before I finally mustered up the courage to talk to my husband about what was going through my head. I shared that I was struggling to find contentment in the servant role I had assumed. I told Charles how I longed to be the "queen" of my home, if only for a day or two.

He looked at me with a little smirk on his face and said, "Honey, you *are* the queen . . . you're a *dairy* queen!" (I'm still nursing our son, so the title fit all too well.) At first I pooched out my bottom lip at his response but then decided to laugh!

My perspective was changed that day. The job I have as a mom may not be revered by others; but right now, it is God's call on my life. It is the highest, most influential position I've ever held. And if the only queen I can be right now is a "dairy queen," I'll take it!

When I find myself feeling low about my position in my household, all I have to do is remember that I'm supposed to be modeling Jesus, who came not to be served, but to serve. If He, the King of Kings, would stoop to the lowly position of a servant, why would I think I should be exempt? Scripture tells us that we can expect to live a similar life to His if we desire to follow Him. "Just as the Son of Man did not come to be served, but to serve, and to give his life as a ransom for many" (Matthew 20:28).

We are called to serve. Many times we feel like a queen with no court. Serving won't always feel *good*. It probably won't be *fair*, and it's rarely *fun* by worldly standards. However, when we serve, we can rejoice in the knowledge that we are honoring the King of Kings, who showed us the ultimate sacrifice.

O Mighty King, thank you that you showed us how to serve, even though you deserved to be served. May I serve my family with a willing heart, not begrudging the call. Help me remember that "whoever wants to become great among you must be your servant, and whoever wants to be first must be your slave" (Matthew 20:26–27). Thank you for allowing me to be the servant-queen in my family! In Jesus' name I pray, amen.

MAMA**DRAMA**

"So here's what I want you to do, [with] God helping you: Take your everyday, ordinary life—your sleeping, eating, going-to-work, and walking-around life—and place it before God as an offering. Embracing what God does for you is the best thing you can do for him. Don't become so well-adjusted to your culture that you fit into it without even thinking. Instead, fix your attention on God. You'll be changed from the inside out" (Romans 12:1–2 THE MESSAGE).

From Selfish to Selfless

WHY IS IT hard to serve unselfishly? I have a few theories. Before marriage everybody tells you, "You deserve more than that guy has to offer. Just wait—the right one will come along." As long as you were still dating, you could dump the guy when he didn't act to suit you.

Then marriage came and your beau didn't have to impress you anymore. Not that our husbands are bad—it's just that *catching us* isn't their focus anymore. But now you can't just let him go or send him away. With those two little words, "I do," you move from the world of the selfish to a place requiring you to be selfless. Few of us make the leap right away; it takes time to grow into that state of selflessness. For some of us (like me), it takes longer than others!

Adjusting to marriage is hard enough, but then kids arrive, providing *even more* opportunities to learn selflessness. No longer is your house your own. Before you know it, toys invade every room. Your time is not your own; instead it is spent loving, cleaning, playing, and cooking. And your body is now not just shared with your husband, but also with a nursing baby, or a child hanging on your back, and maybe another one in the womb.

By letting us be moms, it's like God is helping us get a glimpse of what Jesus did when He left heaven to live on earth. Philippians 2:6–7 says: "Being in the very nature God, [Jesus] did not consider equality with God something to be grasped, but made himself nothing, taking the very nature of a servant, being made in human likeness."

Jesus left what was comfortable to sacrifice for us. We moved from living for ourselves (what we wanted to do, what was comfortable to us), to living for others. But just as Jesus didn't hold on to His power, we shouldn't grasp at holding on to our self-sufficiency or think only of our own interests. When we lay those things down and willingly decide to serve, we have never been more like Christ.

Thinking about what He did for me, leaving heaven and dying

a horrible, humiliating death, makes me more willing to serve my family—not only for them but also for *Him*. When Jesus came to earth as one of us, He gave a whole new meaning to the word *selfless*. As moms, our days are full of "kinks" that really stretch us—spit-up (or throw-up), changed plans, uninvited neighbor kids, homes in disarray, unending laundry, broken sleep—the list could go on and on.

How will you serve today? Do you find yourself grasping, trying to hold on to what works best for you? I wish I could say I am always more concerned about the needs of others than myself, but I'd be lying! For me, it depends on the day.

I pray that when those interruptions come our way today, we'll not cling to "what is best for me," but we'll be able to let go as we remember how much Jesus gave up for us. When He gives us the strength to do that, He will also fill us with joy in the process.

Lord, sometimes we are resentful of all our responsibilities. It's easy to look at our mates and feel they aren't doing as much as we are. Forgive us when we put our eyes on them instead of focusing on you. Help us as we adjust from thinking only of ourselves to caring for our husbands and now living unselfishly as we sacrifice and serve our children. You didn't hold on to your rights, Lord. You gave up the most glorious place to make your entrance into the world through a barn. Then you left the world, dying in the most humiliating way, and you did it all for us. Thank you for loving us. Thank you for your example of not flaunting your power or promoting yourself, but for putting value in being a servant. Help us to follow in your footsteps today. We pray this in your name, Jesus. Amen.

MAMA**DRAMA**

When your husband walks through the door today, stop what you're doing and greet him with a smile because of what Jesus did for you.

Write or print this verse and put it on your washing machine or under the toilet lid to remind you when you perform those everyday chores that you're doing it for the Lord:

> "Being in very nature God, [Jesus] did not consider equality with God something to be grasped, but made himself nothing, taking the very nature of a servant, being made in human likeness. And being found in appearance as a man, he humbled himself and became obedient to death—even death on a cross!" (Philippians 2:6–8).

Big-Mouth Mama

*S*HE HAD TO BE so excited; her boys were hanging out with a nice young man. He would be a good influence. In fact, this was no ordinary guy. She believed He was the one that had been promised, the one who would save them all—the Messiah.

And He had chosen her boys, not just one, but both of them! Oh, how her heart swelled with pride! She always knew they were good boys. It was gratifying to see that someone else, a very important someone else, had also noticed their valuable qualities. She decided that it would be good to make sure He knew *how* great they were. We mamas have a hard time letting go of our kids sometimes. She forgot that her little boys were now men.

It's amazing how easy it is to make irrational things seem logical if we mull them over in our minds long enough. Here's what happened. Jesus was talking to His disciples about His coming death. What serious, sobering words they were hearing.

> Then [without invitation] the mother of Zebedee's sons [James and John] came to Jesus with her sons and, kneeling down, asked a favor of him. . . . "Grant that one of these two sons of mine may sit at your right and the other at your left in your kingdom."
> "You don't know what you are asking," Jesus said to them. "Can you drink the cup I am going to drink? . . . To sit at my right or left is not for me to grant. These places belong to those for whom they have been prepared by my Father" (Matthew 20:20–23).

The other ten disciples probably sat there speechless. Resentment set in. They were mad! I can hear them now. "Those mama's boys! She gets 'em by the scruff of the neck and fights their battles for them!" This mama caused trouble for her boys by trying to push them somewhere they shouldn't have been. She rudely interrupted, taking their thoughts off of Jesus and onto themselves.

Jesus patiently called them all back together and put the disciples and this pushy, big-mouth mama back in their places. He showed them the way that things work in God's kingdom.

"Whoever wants to become great among you must be your servant, and whoever wants to be first must be your slave—just as the Son of Man did not come to be served, but to serve, and to give his life as a ransom for many" (Matthew 20:26–28).

As moms, it's easy for us to push our children in the hopes of giving them a head start. We strive to give them every possible opportunity. We want them to have the best schooling, the best place to live, and the best toys to develop their minds. We want to make life good for them.

It's hard for us to let go, allowing them to deal with the consequences of their actions and fight their own battles. But we must. Only when we let go will God be able to promote our kids in the areas He sees fit and according to His perfect timetable.

Our job is to teach them about being a servant. That's what God wants. He isn't concerned that they have tons of fun or that they experience lots of life. His desire is that they learn to serve. He knows that in serving, we all find great joy. So, ask God for ways to let your kids experience the joy of serving and quiet the big-mouth mama inside.

Lord, you know how I hate to see my children get hurt. I don't like seeing them have to face the consequences of their actions. I am sometimes tempted to push them into things that you might not have for them. Help me to back off when necessary. Teach me to let go little by little. Show me the key times that I do need to intervene for the safety and security of my child. Teach me to serve like you did, instead of trying to promote myself and my family. Learning to let go, I pray in Jesus' name, amen.

MAMA**DRAMA**

Instead of signing your kids up for an extra-curricular activity, have a "serving semester." Watch for ways that your children can serve others, such as drawing pictures and delivering them to residents at your local nursing home, sponsoring a child through World Vision, serving at a soup kitchen, or going on a mission trip. Serving helps take the selfishness out of us.

Loving Jesus

By Megan Breedlove

*A note from Breedlove: Jesus didn't say, "Whatever you do for the least of these, I appreciate it." He said, "Whatever you do for the least of these, you do **for me**" (Matthew 25:40).

I started my day early,
Before the room was light.
I lifted my son from his crib
And wished it was still night.
But as I held him close and said,
"Hi Kenneth, precious one,"
I knew that as I greeted him,
I greeted too God's Son.

When my daughter woke up later
Calling, "Mommy! Mommy! Down!"
I picked her up and hugged her
In her worn Elmo nightgown.
I know she felt the closeness
That a mother's touch affords.
I welcomed not just Ellie,
But so, too, the Lord of Lords.

That day, I mixed some formula
And opened jars of peas.
I fixed some "pizza butter" bread
When she grinned and said, "Pleeeeease."
I heated up some leftovers;
I had to nuke them twice.
And when I fed my children,
I was feeding Jesus Christ.

I made some funny faces,
And "played pubzzles" on the floor.
I dressed kitties, ran around outside,
And played with them some more.
We laughed and jumped and tickled,
Making memories to be stored.

When I spent time with my children,
I spent time with my Lord.

I wiped up sticky cereal
And washed the dishes clean.
I straightened, picked up, put away,
And dusted in between.
I did six loads of laundry
And folded it like new.
When I cleaned for my children,
I cleaned for my Savior, too.

When my children were both crying,
I held them in my arms.
I cuddled them and whispered
That I'd keep them safe from harm.
I told them how their Father saved them
With his perfect Lamb.
When I comforted my children,
I comforted I Am.

Later on that evening,
I put them in the bath.
I washed their little bodies
As they kicked around and splashed.
I dried them in soft towels
And put their jammies on.
When I washed my children's feet,
I washed the Holy One.

I cooked and cleaned and rearranged,
Made beds and taught and played.
I made sure that we had food to eat
and that we often prayed.
I died to self.
I made a home from ordinary things
But when I served my children,
I served the King of Kings.

To some, I have done nothing,
But to two, I've done the world.
I made eternal differences
To my precious boy and girl

And to the One who watches over
Every pathway that I've trod.
For when I've loved my precious children,
I've loved Almighty God.[1]

As moms, we are notorious for expecting so much of ourselves: shopping the sales, clipping coupons, scrapbooking our memories, keeping the house spotless, teaching our children all they need to know, always having healthy snacks for them to eat at home or in the car, as well as three healthy meals served right on time. (Never mind the concerns about how we think we should look, how our children should act, and how our spouse feels about his home.)

However, this poem reminded me that *being* there with a loving servant's heart is what's important. If you do nothing else today, be available for your family. That's what they want the most. And in being there and serving your family, you are in turn loving Jesus.

Lord, when we perform our daily tasks, help us to value what we do the way that you do. You value our availability more than all the things we can accomplish. I pray that you'll help us see when we're too busy to just be with our family. Thank you for seeing our servanthood as a direct expression of love for you. In Jesus' name, amen.

MAMA**DRAMA**

When you do any of these things today—folding, washing, dusting, feeding, dressing, playing, kissing, bathing—remember that what you do for the least of these, you are doing for the Lord.

Spills

Spills here, smudges there, dirty fingers, sticky hair . . .
Lord, I work this way without any pay
what good am I doing day to day?

I change dirty diapers, mop the floor
and wash ten loads of clothes
This grandiose title of "Mother and Mom"
seems more like a janitor's role

I wipe runny noses and pick up toys
fifty times a day
I vacuum the floor, close the back door . . .
And hear, "Mom, can all the neighbor kids play?"

But when I slow down and listen
to Your still small voice as I wash a little face
You remind me of Your unending love
as You daily cleanse me by Your grace.

Words and music by Laurie Hilliard
Copyright 1998 *Hold You, Mommy*

Can you relate to the lyrics of this song? As moms, we serve as cooks, maids, janitors, chauffeurs, conflict resolution specialists— the list could go on and on. It seems the chores are unending . . . and most of the time, exhausting and thankless. When it comes to serving our family, it is definitely not about the money, is it? It is not even about a pat on the back, or appreciation from colleagues and loved ones. Most of the time, serving our family is solely about following . . . following Christ's example.

Colossians 3:23–24 reminds us that we must do all we do for the *Lord*. "Whatever you do, work at it with all your heart, as working for the Lord, not for men, since you know that you will receive an inheritance from the Lord as a reward. It is the Lord Christ you are serving." When I can choose to serve my family out of my love for the Lord, and not for any other reason, I am much more content and joyful.

Besides, if my life is supposed to reflect Christ's love, then I am called to a life of sacrifice (primarily to my family). If the King of Kings can perform the lowly duty of washing the disciples' feet, then why would I complain about wiping a little bottom or cleaning the toilet?

As I ponder what Christ did for me, I am humbled and convicted of my negative attitude about serving my family. God's Word clearly commands an attitude of Christlikeness and explains the attitude of our Savior. Let's review the verse from day 2 (Philippians 2:5–8): "Your attitude should be the same as that of Christ Jesus: Who, being in very nature God, did not consider equality with God something to be grasped, but made himself nothing, taking the very nature of a servant being made in human likeness. And being found in appearance as a man, he humbled himself and became obedient to death on a cross!"

So what's it going to be? Are you going to grumble and complain as you serve your family in the mundane tasks of motherhood? Or will you use the opportunity to follow the example of the one who loves you more than you could ever know? Which makes you feel better? It's your choice.

Lord Jesus, thank you for becoming a servant—a servant unto death so that I might live! May I follow your example as I serve my family. Help me to realize that, contrary to the world's belief, becoming a servant is of the highest importance. Forgive me when I grumble and complain instead of rejoicing in the opportunity to serve those I love. Amen.

MAMA**DRAMA**

As your children make messes today, smile. Remember as you clean their messes up that what you're doing is not only a service to your children, but also (more importantly) an act of obedience to the Lord.

Growing Trust

"My Prayer"

Here I am again Lord,
Bowing down before You,
asking You to help me out somehow.
God, You say You know my thoughts
before I even think them,
So you know just what I'm thinking now . . .

**I am tired and O so weary.
Renew my strength, renew my strength.
For when I'm weak, You promise that
You'll be strong
and I need your strength to help me carry on.**

"My Prayer" by Laurie Hilliard
Hold You, Mommy 1998

"When I Am Afraid"

WHEN ALEC, my oldest son, was three years old, he had to have hernia surgery. Only a few months earlier, our little guy had endured another surgery; he'd had tubes put in his ears for the second time. Even though it had been a minor surgery, it was a stressful experience. The trauma of the nurses taking him out of my arms was still a disturbing memory. I was determined to make the next hospital visit a little more bearable for all of us.

So I phoned the hospital ahead of time and talked with the pediatric nurse. When I explained our situation, she assured me that right before surgery they would give Alec some "happy" medicine, and it would make him as loopy as loopy could be! I was thrilled to hear that, and much less troubled about the upcoming surgery after talking to her.

The day finally arrived. We drove our little guy to the hospital early that morning. He was happy and cheerful. Not long after we arrived, the nurse came in. She had a little cup of the "loopy" medicine and assured us that it would take effect shortly. It wasn't even ten minutes before it began to work. Alec started reaching for things in the air. He was talking silly, and his eyes looked as if he were on drugs. (I guess he was, wasn't he?)

A short while later we pulled him down to the surgery holding area in a little red wagon. Charles and I were laughing uncontrollably as we watched our little boy's strange behavior. He was still reaching for unseen objects in the air when we rounded a corner. We thought for sure we were going to lose him over the edge of the wagon!

We sat in the holding room as we waited for the nurses to come and take him to surgery. Slowly, one by one, all of the other patients were taken away. We were still waiting. After thirty minutes had passed, Alec's medicine began to wear off, and the doctor still hadn't arrived. He was late. I was getting worried, so I asked the nurse if he could have some more "loopy" juice. She said that they couldn't give him any more because by then it was too close to his surgery. My heart sank in my chest.

Alec became aware of what was going on. He asked if I would hold him, then he crawled out of the little red wagon and into my lap. Tears began to well up in my eyes. How small he looked in his little hospital gown. He sat in my lap for a few moments before he asked, "Can we sing when I am afwaid?"

I knew immediately what Alec meant. We had been listening to Steve Green's Scripture tapes at home, and we'd learned a praise song taken directly from Psalm 56:3–4. That's what my son wanted to sing. I answered, "Yes, buddy. We sure can." Trying my best not to cry, I began singing with him, "When I am afraid, I will trust in you . . . In God, whose word I praise." [1]

I kept holding him close. It wasn't long before the nurses finally came and took him into surgery. He cried and so did I. I remember thinking, "Lord, why did this have to happen? I did everything to keep my baby from experiencing fear, but even my best efforts were not enough."

I didn't receive an answer right away, but several months later the lesson in it all became very clear. I realized that *I'm not always going to be there* to comfort and protect my children. They need to know to Whom they can *always go* when they are afraid. Fortunately, my three-year-old already knew. After he climbed into my lap, Alec knew he needed to go to God when he was "afwaid." What a great reminder it was for me.

What about you? Are you afraid? Are your fears leaving you too paralyzed to be the mom that you want to be? Do your fearful thoughts sometimes consume you? Do you know where to go when you are afraid? In 1 Peter 5:7 we are encouraged to "Cast all your anxiety on him because he cares for you." Go to God. When you are "afwaid" you can trust in Him.

Prince of Peace, pour your Spirit over me in this very moment. Let me rest in your love, which casts out all fear. Thank you that you never sleep or tire of my coming to you. When I am afraid, help me remember I can trust in you. In the name of Jesus I make my requests known. Amen.

MAMA**DRAMA**

Hide God's Word in your heart in creative ways: listen to Scriptures put to music. Post God's Word on the "doorposts" of your house. Frame Bible verses and put them on your wall.

Here I Am, Lord. I'm Listening

*A*T BREAKFAST one morning we were reading from our children's Bible (one of God's favorite ways to speak to my heart). The story went something like this: After going to bed, Samuel thought he heard Eli calling him. He went to him, saying, "Here I am." He went three times before Eli realized that Samuel wasn't just trying to keep him awake—God was speaking to the boy. So Eli told Samuel, "Next time answer, 'Speak, Lord, for your servant is listening'" (1 Samuel 3:9).

It hit me that God didn't say anything further until Samuel answered, "Your servant is listening." I'm so busy, sometimes even busy with godly stuff, that I put God off. Sometimes I don't answer "Here I am" or stop to listen because I'm too busy to hear. But at other times I don't answer because I'm afraid.

While writing this book I have gone through a time of wanting to answer, "Here am I, Lord," but I've been gripped with fear. I couldn't figure out why I was so worried about trusting Him and putting my life into His hands. After all, He is so much more capable to control my life than I am, and is ultimately in control of my every breath.

It wasn't that I couldn't look back and see how faithful He had been through the years. Time after time He has led me in ways that I never would have gone without His prompting. I knew that I could trust Him for the days ahead, but *knowing* about His faithfulness and actually *trusting* Him are two different things.

My greatest fear was that one of my children would die. I was afraid if I fully surrendered to Him, He would allow one of them to be taken from us. The fear persisted. I talked to Laurie about it, and she said, "Why is it that we think surrendering to God means something *bad* is going to happen?"

It must be a common thought for mothers. I remember our own mom telling us something that she frequently thought: "Things are so good, I wonder what is about to happen." How foolish we are to even think such worried thoughts! Just because things are good, or just because we surrender, doesn't mean anything in and of itself.

I can't let these negative ideas keep me from the very thing that is best for me. If I never say, "Here I am," or if I never stop to listen, I won't hear what my Father wants to tell me. I'll miss out on the plans He has and the strength He gives for the trying days.

Have you been struggling with giving everything without reservation to Him? What makes you nervous? Probably some of the same fears I had. Just because you surrender doesn't mean something bad is going to happen to your family. At the same time, just because you answer, "Here I am," you're not guaranteed that bad things won't happen. The real choice has to do with something far more important: whether we will be familiar with God's strength and help, no matter what comes.

Which would you rather do: carry the burdens of life on your own, or hold on to the Lord as He carries them for you? Maybe your heart is resistant like mine was . . . and sometimes still is. The psalmist said, "Pushed to the wall, I called to God; from the wide open spaces, he answered. God's now at my side and I'm not afraid; who would dare lay a hand on me?" (Psalm 118:5–6 THE MESSAGE). Answer Him today, "Here I am. Speak, Lord . . . I'm listening."

Lord, you are trustworthy. I can say that, but sometimes it's hard to live my days believing it. Forgive me, Lord. I need you more than anything. Help me hold on to the truth of your Word. You care so deeply about me. Please take away the fear of surrendering that causes me to stagger in my trust. Thank you for never letting go of me. Help me follow you every day, instead of trying to run my life my way. You are far more capable. Here I am, Lord. Open my ears to hear what you want to say. Trusting you, more and more, because of Jesus. In His name I pray, amen.

MAMA**DRAMA**

Today when your kids call your name, answer, "Here I am, I'm listening." It will remind you to trust the Lord all day, and you might even get to explain the story of Samuel to your kids. You can find the story in 1 Samuel 3:2–18.

Stormy Weather

MY SON ALEC, who is now eleven, has always been afraid of storms. He doesn't like to hear thunder. He can't stand a torrential rain and doesn't find amusement in a beautiful lightning show. He simply doesn't like storms of any kind. If there is the slightest hint that we may have bad weather, he wants to either monitor the weather channel on TV or watch the radar on *weather.com*. He sometimes obsesses about it all. It is a very real fear for him.

One night, several years ago, (when Alec was much younger) there was a pretty bad thunderstorm. It was so loud that it awakened him from his sleep. He was terrified. He came running into our room, crying as another loud clap of thunder rattled the pictures on the walls. I lifted him into our bed and placed him between my husband and me. I moved close to him and wrapped my arms around him. He immediately fell asleep.

My husband and I looked at each other and laughed at how quickly he'd gone back to sleep. It was because he felt safe and secure. The thunder got louder and lightning illuminated our whole room, but Alec kept sleeping! I was amazed. He was the perfect picture of peace.

Thinking of my son lying there sleeping peacefully through the storm reminded me of someone else who slept peacefully through a storm. The storm on the sea was raging, and Jesus (the Prince of Peace) was sleeping through it.

In our lives, we too will face stormy weather. Is the water getting so rough you feel you are about to drown? Maybe you have a sick child, a husband who is a workaholic, a special-needs child, or a job loss. You may be a single mom or a mom of a rebellious teen. Perhaps you are passing through the storms of sorrow because you've experienced a devastating loss in your life.

Whatever the stormy weather looks like in your life, you can experience a peace that passes all understanding. How? By drawing near to the Prince of Peace who dwells in you. I love Philippians 4:7: "And the peace of God, which transcends all understanding, will guard your hearts and your minds in Christ Jesus."

I like to think of it like this: When I am afraid or worried, I call out to God, who reaches down and draws me close. He wraps His protective, loving arms around me, and I fall asleep, finding peace in the midst of my "stormy weather."

> *Prince of Peace, calm my spirit right now. Remind me that instead of worrying, I need to be praying. Draw me close to you, O Lord. For in you I will find perfect peace even when the storms are raging around me. Thank you that I can trust you even in the midst of the storms to keep me safe, secure, and sleeping. Good night, Lord; I'm sleeping tight in your arms tonight. Amen.*

MAMA**DRAMA**

When your children come to you because they're afraid, pray with them and then hold them tightly. As you help calm their fears, thank God that He is the Prince of Peace in life's stormy weather.

The next time a thunderstorm comes your way, read with your children the story about Jesus calming the storm in Luke 8:22–25.

The Worrywart

*D*ON'T WORRY." It sounds so easy, but it's easier said than done. Why is it so difficult not to worry? Probably because worry is a human reaction to circumstances that are out of our control. Often, worry is a symptom of underlying fear. You've experienced it, and so have I.

Before I became a mom I worried some, but after I had children I worried a lot! I took worry to a whole new level—I became a worrywart. I remember experiencing irrational fears. Weird thoughts would flit through my mind, causing me to worry. "What if I do something crazy, like forget the baby is in the car?" Or "What if I can't tell when something is wrong with my baby? What if my kids get hurt when I'm not around? What if something happens to me? What if something happens to them? What if my husband loses his job? What if my kids don't turn out like I think they should?" Or "What if I really can't do this mothering thing?"

Sometimes the worries seem to be strung together, one right after the other, like diapers pulled from a Diaper Genie. In those early years of parenting, there were times I was completely paralyzed by worry and fear. They would almost consume me.

During those times I would reason with myself, trying to convince "me" that I wasn't being sensible. Attempting to dismiss the unfounded thoughts, I would busy myself with anything I could find. Still, no matter how hard I tried, the worrisome feelings found their way back into the corners of my mind. Fear would again grip my soul.

Finally I realized that I was no match for this enemy called "worry." On my own, I was incapable of winning the battle that was raging in my mind. I needed God to free me from this prison of worry in which I was trapped.

I went to His Word and read in Matthew 6:31–32, "So do not worry, saying, 'What shall we eat?' or 'What shall we drink?' or 'What shall we wear?' For the pagans run after all these things, and your heavenly Father knows that you need them." Here's our part: "But seek first his kingdom and his righteousness, and all these things will be given to you as well. Therefore do not worry about tomorrow, for tomorrow will worry about itself. Each day has enough trouble of its own" (Matthew 6:33–34).

God reminded me that He cared so deeply for me that I didn't need to worry. He was able to take good care of me! THE MESSAGE interprets verse 34 this way: "Give your entire attention to what God is doing right now, and don't get worked up about what may or may not happen tomorrow. God will help you deal with whatever hard things come up when the time comes."

Focus on God instead of your fear. When we seek Him first (filling our minds with His truth), we will be able to trust Him better with all that holds us captive. We can trust Him. He takes care of birds (Matthew 6:26), so why would we think He won't take care of us? If you are a worrywart, focus on Him. Read His Word and lay your worries at His feet.

> *God of all comfort, I confess—I have wasted much of my energy worrying. At times I am so afraid, Lord. You invite us to cast our anxiety on you because you care for us. Let your words sink deep into my soul. May I really believe what you say. You care for me. I can trust you. I don't want to live a life of fear any longer. I want to be free from the grip of worry. In this very moment I choose to put my trust in you. I am laying down my worries at your feet. You are able to bear their burden, so I no longer have to do so. Thank you for making my load lighter. I love you. Amen.*

MAMA**DRAMA**

Listen to Christian music. It is food for the soul. It also helps you focus on God instead of your circumstances.

Write down your fears. Say the words out loud. Place them in an envelope with *God* printed on the outside.

Memorize some Scriptures pertaining to fear so you can recall them when the situation arises. Here are some suggestions: 1 John 4:18, Deuteronomy 31:8, Hebrews 13:5b, Matthew 28:20b, John 14:27.

Faith Walking

W E WALK BY faith, not by sight" (2 Corinthians 5:7 NASB). I read the words, but what caught my eye wasn't the verse. It was how nicely the words were inscribed on a decorative sign. I decided the plaque, painted in the exact colors of my kitchen, was a perfect fit and worth the money. Besides, I liked having Scripture displayed in my home. I thought how fitting the words were for our family because my husband had quit his job a few years ago to work full time in this ministry to moms. Yes, I was certain that we were *the example* of walking by faith.

We hung the sign above our pantry door as a reminder that our family walks by faith. One day, when the financial struggles were heaped on the shoulders of my husband and me like a grown elephant, I leaned against my counter in a huff.

How would we make things work? There wasn't even enough money in the ministry bank account to pay us for the next pay period. What about our cars? They are both falling apart. What if we had to replace one of them? How could we afford it? And what about this conference that's coming up? People haven't registered and we'll be out lots of money with the hotel if enough people don't attend.

As I stood in my kitchen, paralyzed by my worries and fears, my eyes met the sign—*We walk by faith. Ha!* I thought. *Maybe when things were going well!* I was humbled to see how fragile my faith truly was. It's easy to trust God when we can make the plans and see where we're going.

I remember one night sharing with some trusted friends at church about my financial fears. I told them, "I can look back and see how God has been faithful. It's just that I'm struggling with things right now."

A sweet lady interpreted my own words: "If you can look back and see God's faithfulness in situations that were once unclear, don't you think one day you'll look back to this time and see His faithfulness here too?" Faith is not something that I don't have proof of; it's just that I don't have it in advance. The faith I had in past circumstances is now evidenced by the facts of today.

Trusting that God will do what He says He will do . . . that is faith. He promised to supply all of our needs (Philippians 4:19). So we can stop worrying and trust Him. Our hope is in Him, not in what we can see. "For what is seen is temporary, but what is unseen is eternal" (2 Corinthians 4:18).

My hope wasn't going to be found in our finances (the temporary), but in the Lord (the eternal). "Command those who are rich . . . not to . . . put their hope in wealth, which is so uncertain, but to put their hope in God, who richly provides us with everything" (1 Timothy 6:17–19).

Are you walking by faith, or are you trying to see what is next? Maybe you are worried about your finances, an illness in the family, or a child who is struggling in school. Perhaps you are dealing with an uncertain job situation or an unstable family relationship. If so, go to the Lord. Walk with Him. Have faith in Him, for "he who promised is faithful" (Hebrews 10:23).

> *Lord, I am quick to trust you on the good days, but the uncertain days can leave me in a panic. It's no shock to you that I've been worrying about* _____
>
> _____
>
> _____
>
> _____.
>
> *Help me walk by faith and not waste my time trying to figure things out. I know there are some things that I'm not supposed to see yet. I know I can trust you. Help me to not just know it, but also live it by giving my worries to you. Enable me to believe that you will do what you promised. Please give me your peace. Learning to walk by faith, amen.*

MAMA**DRAMA**

Lead your kids around the house with a blindfold over their eyes. Spin them around, then have them guess where they are. Let them do the same thing to you. You can tell them, "Sometimes in life, it's like we have a blindfold over our eyes, and we can't see where we're going. Just as we guided each other, God is there to guide us and show us the way. We don't have to wander alone in the dark." Thank God together and ask Him to help your family learn to walk by faith every day.

Hanging On to Hope

"We know that suffering produces perseverance;
perseverance, character;
and character, hope.
And hope does not disappoint us,
because God has poured out his love into our hearts
by the Holy Spirit, whom he has given us."

Romans 5:3–5

Sugarland

SEVERAL YEARS ago we were headed to Sugarland, Texas. I asked the kids to draw what they thought it was going to be like. My oldest daughter really got into it and drew candy buildings and castles of sugar—a real kid's dreamland. To say the least, she was more than a little disappointed when we arrived to find that it was just another city. (Nothing against Sugarland, for those of you who live there. The people there are as sweet as they can be!)

When I think about sugarcoating, that is what it is—a coating of sugar that looks very appealing on the outside. It's hard to realize that life is only sugar *coated.* Marriage isn't as syrupy as it started out to be, the kids aren't always sweet, and sometimes life is like a box of melted chocolates—sort of sweet, but kinda messy!

John 16:33b says: "In this world you will have trouble. But take heart! I have overcome the world." Spills, stains, and breaks will happen. Plans will change and expectations will fail, but our hope is in the One who has overcome the world. The Bible says, "He . . . put his Spirit in our hearts as a deposit, guaranteeing what is to come" (2 Corinthians 1:22).

In all of our roles—as moms, wives, and women—our minds have to deal with earthly things like moldy who-knows-what in the fridge, mud on the carpet, or traffic jams. Maybe you have a husband who is less than involved in the kids' lives or a mother-in-law who seemingly has all the answers.

Life definitely has its problems, and we all have to live with the struggles. But as believers in Christ, we don't have to *drown* in them. "There's far more to life for us. We're citizens of high heaven!" (Philippians 3:20 THE MESSAGE).

Life is going to be sour sometimes. We can choose, however, to keep trusting Him in the hard times, knowing that heaven will be pure joy and sweetness like we've never tasted before. As followers of Jesus Christ, the hope we have is not in this life, it's in Him!

Heaven is something about which we can be joyful. I was

always worried that if I talked to my children about heaven, one of us would surely die soon after. Finally I realized that I was just being superstitious. Talking to our kids (or any fellow Christian) about heaven is a great way to share our hope in Christ. One mom told me as we were leaving an event, "If I don't see you before, I'll see you in heaven." What a sweet reminder!

If this place (earth) doesn't feel very homey at times, it's because we're not really home. Heaven is our Sugarland, where we'll meet Jesus face to face. I'm excited about going "home," where there are no more complaints or comparisons, no more deadlines, no more fund-raisers, no more tears, and no more hurts. We will have time to sit and drink coffee (I'll be having iced tea) for as long as we like about how gracious God has been to us. Things that seem out of focus on earth will be seen clearly.

The Bible says that Jesus has gone to prepare a place for us there in heaven. (In today's décor-conscious lingo, we would call that a "space"!) Maybe you can't afford a personal decorator now, but wow—just think! In your heavenly space you have access to the designer who created every flower, every bird, and every sunset—the One who created you!

Jesus knows the desires of our hearts, so I'm guessing I'll have a log cabin/lodge type place with really big trees out the windows. And I think my daughter might have a "Sugarland Castle" beyond anything she could ever imagine! There's no place like home!

> *Lord, you are so gracious. You not only gave us your Son to cover our sins, but you have gone above and beyond anything we can comprehend. You have given us your Spirit in this life and have gone on to prepare a place for us when we have taken our last breath. Thank you for thinking it all out for us, and for loving us enough to want to have us with you for an eternity! I praise you that there's far more to life for us. "We're citizens of high heaven!" Thank you for walking with us each day we live on this earth. We look forward to our time with you in heaven. You are an awesome God, worthy of our praise. In Jesus' name I pray, amen.*

MAMA**DRAMA**

If you need an art project today, let your kids draw what they think heaven will be like.

When you pay your house payment, home insurance, or rent each month, let it be a reminder of your real home . . . the one with no mortgage or other expenses.

Run!

HAVE YOU EVER thought God was speaking to you? Did you quickly dismiss the idea thinking, "That can't be God. It doesn't make any sense"? Don't be so sure! Isaiah 55:9 reminds us, "My ways [are] higher than your ways and my thoughts [are higher] than your thoughts." God's truths and His ways may not always seem logical to us.

As I read God's Word, I find it very interesting that God used the most unlikely people and unusual circumstances at times to carry out His plans and purposes. Think of David, for example. He was a common shepherd boy, but God had another plan for him— to defeat the Philistine army by killing a giant (Goliath) with a stone and slingshot! No one would have ever believed David could pull that off. Scripture tells us that David knew he wasn't capable, but God would give him victory over Goliath. Not only did David kill a giant in an unusual way, but God chose him to be Israel's king! Go figure.

Then there was Joseph, who was sold into slavery by his jealous brothers. God had a bigger plan for him too. He moved Joseph from prison to become the right-hand man to Pharaoh. Who would've thought? The list of improbable people and bizarre situations could go on and on. It just goes to show—don't ever negate a nudge from the Lord simply because it doesn't make sense to you!

Not long ago my friend Cynthia shared an interesting story with me. She was diagnosed with thyroid cancer ten years ago. Surgery removed her thyroid, and extensive radiation treatments followed. Complications ensued and Cynthia's recovery was slow. Finding the appropriate medication proved to be a real challenge.

Two years after her surgery, my friend continued to feel horrible. Taking care of two young children in the midst of her illness was taking its toll. She had no energy, no stamina, and no motivation. She simply didn't feel well.

She went to medical doctors, who told her she was depressed. She thought that was a little odd, but she went to see a psychiatrist just in case they were right. He prescribed medication. Still nothing helped. In desperation, she cried out to God, "Lord, let me die if I'm going to continue to feel like this."

That's when she sensed God's Spirit speak to her. He said, **"Run."** "Run?" she questioned. "What does that have to do with anything? I don't have the energy to run!" Because it didn't make sense to her, my friend dismissed the idea. However, the thought would not go away. For three years God's quiet voice patiently prodded her, **"Run, just run."**

Finally Cynthia realized that she had to make radical changes to take care of herself. She quit her job and reluctantly gave in to God's nudging. My friend put on her running shoes and headed out the door. She was gonna run!

Even after she gave in to God's prodding, she wasn't totally convinced that this was the answer. Running didn't feel good. She didn't really like it, but she relentlessly obeyed. She kept running. Shortly after the soreness subsided, something else began to happen. Gradually, Cynthia started to feel better. Her body was healing! The gloom of depression was being lifted like an early morning fog, dissolving in the sunshine.

Has God been nudging your spirit? Whether it makes sense to you or not, *heed His call.* He can be trusted. God knows you better than you know yourself. He wants the best for you. Put on your figurative running shoes, head out the door, and "Run!"

> *Lord, I want to hear your voice. Help me to trust you even when I can't see the whole plan. I want to be obedient to your call. Lead me—I want to follow. Thank you for the hope I have in Christ. In His name I pray, amen.*

MAMADRAMA

Because moms are pulled in every direction, needed by everyone, often isolated, exhausted, and sleep deprived, depression is quite common. Many times the demands on a woman's life are a perfect recipe for a bad case of "the blues."

Don't try to go this road alone. Find a friend with whom you can share your burden.

If you are struggling with depression, or simply feeling unmotivated and down, you might try exercising. Specifically, running. It has been medically proven that running is helpful in alleviating depression. Try it!

Living in the Sonshine

L AST YEAR, when I experienced the sorrow of a miscarriage, I experienced new depths of sadness, anger, and hopelessness. I found myself feeling irritable and impatient with those I loved, and I became increasingly unmotivated and depressed. It was a very challenging time in my life.

Trusting God when we can't seem to make sense of things is very difficult. As I wandered aimlessly through this grim time in my life, I found myself crying out to God. My heart was so heavy, and life as I had known it seemed pointless.

I remember sitting at home in a grief-induced gloom, numbly turning the pages in my Bible. I was searching for answers, desperately looking for comfort. At first, I began reading in Job (now, there is a fellow who experienced heartache). Then I turned to Psalm 139.

I was familiar with this passage. I had memorized it when I was in college. But as I read it again, the words began to jump off the page in a whole new way. The first few verses told of how God knew everything about me. As I continued reading, I was reminded that there was *no place* I could go to hide from God's Spirit.

The verses that seemed to reach out and grab me the most were verses 11–12, which said, "If I say, 'Surely the darkness will hide me and the light become night around me,' even the darkness will not be dark to you; the night will shine like the day, for darkness is as light to you."

Suddenly I realized that no matter how dark it seemed around me, *my darkness could not consume God.* Even in the darkest times in life, God's light is always shining. God used His Word that day to hold me close and comfort me.

Have you ever boarded an airplane on a dark, cloudy day? Maybe when it was raining or snowing? One terribly dreary day my plane left the ground. When we entered the clouds, the ride became a little rough. The plane seemed to churn as it passed through the storm. It was dark outside my window.

However, in only a few short moments, the turbulence stopped. The plane felt as if it were simply floating. Then, a most remarkable sight came into view. The darkness melted away and the sun, which had been hidden only a few minutes before, was shining so brightly that it was blinding. Even though below the clouds it was dark and gloomy, the sun had been shining—I just couldn't see it.

That is the way it is with God. Sometimes we may not "feel" His presence because our world is so dark, but He is shining His light all the same. "Darkness will not be dark to you." Praise be to God! I don't know what is causing your "darkness" today, but be assured that God will not be consumed by it. "The night will shine like the day." Hold on to Him and your days will be bright again.

Father, I am hurting; my burdens of sorrow and grief are heavy. I am angry. I don't understand why this is happening. My world seems hopeless right now. Thank you, Lord, that even though my world is consumed with darkness, yours is not. It cannot be. I will hold on to you, for you are the light that can pull me out of my darkness. When I can't see what's above the clouds, I'll still trust you. Amen.

MAMA**DRAMA**

If you are grieving, try recording your feelings in a journal. Sometimes writing out your thoughts and feelings can help you process them better. Read Psalm 139 and let it minister to your heart.

Find someone who will listen to your story as many times as you need to tell it.

Another Dream

ſEVERAL YEARS ago Charles and I were itching to build a new house. We deemed our house too small—even though it had three bedrooms, two baths, a living room, dining room, large kitchen, two-car garage, and storage space in the attic. We were eager and excited, searching through house magazines for the perfect floor plan. It needed to have a large great room, more closet space, and a spacious laundry room. And, of course, we wanted lots of trees on a two- or three-acre lot!

Daily my thoughts were consumed with thoughts of my "dream home." Even mundane tasks like washing dishes, picking up toys, and making dinner all seemed a little less burdensome as my mind wandered to thoughts of my future home.

We put our house up for sale, and things began to move quickly. Our house sold in only three weeks. We ended up moving in with my ninety-year-old grandmother while waiting to find or build our dream home.

I didn't know it at the time, but the dream I believed would bring me happiness was far different from the dream God had planned for my life. Shortly after moving in with Granny, it became obvious that our plans were going to change. God was calling Sharon and me to speak more, which would include traveling with our husbands and children for months at a time.

The hopes of building a dream home were gone. Instead, we would be buying a small double-wide mobile home to be moved in behind my grandmother's home. We were also purchasing two older forty-foot buses to be converted into motor homes in which we would live and travel while on the road. Each bus would have less than three hundred square feet of living space . . . talk about downsizing! Charles and I went from living in seventeen hundred square feet to less than three hundred square feet. God does have a sense of humor!

As I look back over the past four years, at the time I've spent with my family traveling across the United States to encourage moms, I'm amazed by God's hand in it all. He had a wonderful plan—one I would never have imagined. And to think I would have missed it if I had not given up *my dream* for His dream.

Many times we hold on to our own dreams, believing that we will find happiness in them. But true happiness comes when our dreams line up with God's plan for our lives. You can trust Him. Don't hold on to something so tightly that you miss God's best for you!

God has good plans for you. Jeremiah 29:11 states it well: " 'For I know the plans I have for you,' declares the Lord, 'plans to prosper you and not to harm you, plans to give you hope and a future.' " God loves you so much and He wants to give you the best. Trust Him.

I never could have imagined what God had in store when I trusted Him with my dreams. He made my dreams come true— Charles and I do have a "dream home." It's just not quite what we expected. That forty-foot, fifteen-ton, purple piece of metal has become a dream home for now. I can't tell you the peace that has come from submitting to His plan for our lives.

> *Lord, I know you are my Provider. You know what I need better than I do. May your dreams become mine. I want to desire the things you do. Father, you know that I've been dreaming about* _____ _____ _____ _____. *Show me if this is your plan and purpose for me. Reveal your dreams for my life. Thank you for your faithfulness. "Now to him who is able to do immeasurably more than all we ask or imagine, according to his power that is at work within us, to him be glory in the church and in Christ Jesus throughout all generations, for ever and ever! Amen"* (Ephesians 3:20).

MAMA**DRAMA**

Write a list of things you dream about. Pray about each item on the list. Ask God to show you if this is your dream alone, or if it is a part of His divine plan for your life. Listen and obey as He reveals the answer. You won't be disappointed.

Hold On

I WANTED HER to hold on to my hand as we crossed the street, but she was holding her stuffed animal in one hand and her lollipop in the other. She thought about it, then stuck the sucker in her mouth, freeing up a hand to grab mine.

Later on, as Pat (my husband) prayed, I didn't hear a word he said. I had the weight of indecision in one hand and the heaviness of discontentment in the other. Rather than holding on to the promises of the Lord, I was clawing for answers.

Are we in the right place to raise our children? Is our church the right fit for us as a family? Are we finding the right balance between giving our children opportunities and not giving them everything? What are we going to do about not having enough money? What will we do if one of our paid-for but ancient vehicles decides to quit?

I was in a really prayerful mode, as you can tell! In all my questions, my heart was crying out to God. *Hold on to me* was the thought that flew through my head. All through the rest of the day, when I began worrying, *Hold on to me* kept coming to my mind.

Why should I let go of my worries so I can hold on to Him? Because everything else in life changes except Him . . . everything! Think about it. Houses fall apart, cars start out new but eventually grow old, our bodies change, kids change, and places change. But God is the same today as He was yesterday, and He'll still be the same tomorrow and the next day and forever (Hebrews 13:8). Psalm 102:27 says, "You remain the same, and your years will never end."

Nothing in life will ever be perfect. Our house will never be exactly what we want, our church won't do everything the way we think things should be done, we will make mistakes raising our children, and money will come and go, but in all of the change, God is the same, and He will meet our needs (Philippians 4:19). In every situation, God is still God.

As we conclude this study, I know that all the problems

haven't been erased from your life. You could still be struggling with indecision about your mothering. You could feel like your marriage is crumbling around you. You might be financially unable to do many of the things that you want/need to do . . . maybe including just paying your bills.

Don't try to hold it all together, Mom. If something is in your hand, it's hard to hold His hand. Just as our kids say, "Hold you, Mommy," God wants to hold us. If God is the only thing that remains the same, why wouldn't we let go of the circumstances that constantly change and hold on to Him?

What are you clinging to that you need to let go of so you can keep a firm grip on His promises? He is faithful. Put the lollipops of life somewhere else and hold on to Him. You are safe in His arms. He will never let you go.

Lord, please show me how to hold on to you. Sometimes I want to hold on to you, but I don't know how to let go of the things in life so that I can take hold of you. Show me, Lord. I want to let go of . . . _____

_____

_____

_____

_____

Thank you for keeping me safe in your arms. I ask all of this in Jesus' name, amen.

MAMA**DRAMA**

Mark Matthew 11:28 in your Bible. Read it several times. I pray that you will find rest as you read it. This verse is an amazing gift. In case you don't have a Bible available, here it is in two different versions:

"Come to me, all you who are weary and burdened, and I will give you rest."

"Are you tired? Worn out? Burned out on religion? Come to me. Get away with me and you'll recover your life. I'll show you how to take a real rest" (THE MESSAGE).

Leader's Guide

Dear Leader,

Thank you for the time that you are investing in these moms. We wish that we could be there with you in person each week! We pray that you will be encouraged and that your times together will be life changing. We would love to hear your stories. Feel free to email us at: *mail@momandlovingit.org.*

We thought it might be helpful to give you an informal plan for the group meeting. You could do something like:

1. Open in prayer. (Be cautious not to call on someone to pray unless you asked them privately beforehand.)
2. Use the activities provided in the following pages, or something else you think would work.
3. Ask someone to share how they used one or more of the Mama Drama ideas.
4. Discuss the questions for the week (see following pages).
5. Talk about a verse that meant a lot and what they felt God was teaching them through it.
6. Close in prayer. (Feel free to use a prayer given or pray your own.)
7. Invite them to copy the verse you are assigning for the next week.

Of course, you could always have snacks somewhere in that plan! We hope this time of getting together with other women is truly a blessing to you.

Following Him,
Sharon and Laurie

Week 1: He's Always There

Preparation: Bring or purchase *Hold You, Mommy* (available at *www.momandlovingit.org*. All the songs used during the study are on the CD). Choose a verse from week 2 to memorize. Write it on an index card or on a dry-erase board. Bring index cards and markers for the moms to copy the verse.

Note to Leader: For some moms, the thought of God as a father figure may be difficult because their relationship with their father wasn't a positive one. Be sensitive as you discuss His love, gentleness, and kindness. This may be someone's first introduction to the Lord. Make them feel comfortable and welcome by using common language, not "Christianese" (avoid words like Holy Ghost or Holy Spirit, redemption, salvation, born again, etc.).

Activity: Play "Hold You, Mommy" (track 7)

Questions:
1. What made the most impact on you this week as you read?
2. What was your relationship like with your earthly father?
3. How does it affect the way you view your heavenly Father?
4. How does God show you He loves you?
5. How does knowing that God never sleeps make you feel about Him?
6. Is it hard for you to believe God could love you unconditionally?

Closing: Read aloud "Remembertations." (Appendix 2)
Encourage the moms to copy the Bible verse and put it in a prominent spot so they can see it each day.

*If you don't already have the names, email addresses, and numbers (including cell phone numbers) of the moms in your group, get those before they leave. You'll need them for an activity later.

Week 2: Comfort in the Chaos

Preparations: Pick up "troll" pencils (the ones with the wild hair) for each mom. Choose a key verse for moms to memorize from week 3; collect index cards and markers.

Activity: Hand out "troll" pencils to each mom. All together, roll the pencil between your hands and see how many of your ladies can relate to the troll! This week's topic will probably be an easy discussion if they will open up. They will be more likely to be open and honest if you are vulnerable with them about your struggles in this area.

Questions:
1. What makes you most angry?
2. Make a list of the things that exhaust and overwhelm you. How can you alleviate some of the stress?
3. What do you do when you "lose it" with your kids?
4. Have you forgiven yourself?

Week 3: Getting to Know God

Preparations: Choose a key verse from week 4; collect index cards and markers.

Note to Leader: Because your moms will be at different spiritual levels in their relationship with the Lord, this week can be crucial in leading them to spend time with Him. The idea isn't to make them feel guilty for not investing in their relationship, but to help them see the many ways that they can develop that relationship with God—and the benefits of doing so.

Activity: Have each mom write down something about themselves that others would not know. (If it's a small group, they can write two things.) Put them together in a hat. Then let each mom pull one of the pieces of paper out of a hat and guess who wrote it. Point out how we get to know one another by spending time together and listening to each other, and mention that it will be the same with our relationship with Christ.

Questions:
1. Have you studied God's Word (the Bible) in the past?
2. What do you feel you need to do to have a "legitimate" quiet time? Do you feel pressure to make it legitimate?
3. How has your view of getting to know God changed this week?
4. Which ideas did you try, if any, to deepen your relationship with the Lord?

Week 4: Expecting Too Much

Preparations: Bring magazines that have great covers (elegant homes, mouth-watering foods, perfect bodies, stunning faces, adorable children, etc.), a verse from week 5, markers, and index cards.

Activity: As you show the magazines, ask the moms, "How does this make you feel when you look at it?" Talk about how we compare ourselves to what looks perfect.

Questions:
1. When do you expect too much of yourself?
2. Tell about a time when you had expectations of your spouse that were not realistic.
3. Do you sometimes expect too much from your children (emotionally, physically, mentally, and spiritually)?
4. On what do you "dwell"?

Week 5: Contentment—It's Your Choice

Preparations: *Hold You, Mommy* CD and player, a verse from week 6, markers, and index cards.

Activity: When you think about your life right now, what is causing you the most discontentment? Is it the lack of energy, a messy house, or sibling rivalry between your kids? Now "fast forward" ten years. Will you miss some of these things?

Questions:
1. In what area of your life are you most discontent?
2. Why does discontentment steal our joy?
3. How are you choosing to "stay" discontent? Or how are you moving toward contentment?
4. What can you do to change your perspective of the situation?

Closing: Listen to "These Days" (track 10). Feel free to listen to the song earlier if you want.

Week 6: Livin' It

Preparations: Flashlights from a dollar store, verse for week 7, and markers.

Activity: Give each mom a small keychain flashlight (from a dollar store). Tell them to remember when they use the flashlight that, with God's help, they can let their light shine in their family.

Questions:
1. What have you heard your children say and immediately thought, *That sounds just like me?*
2. What do you need to work on because you know your children are watching?
3. How does having a child change the way you talk and what you do?
4. What are the positive things you would like to pass down to your children?

Optional for close of meeting: Turn off the light and let them turn on their flashlights one at a time as you all sing "This Little Light of Mine."

Week 7: Reflections

Preparations: Make a copy of Appendix 3, "Who Am I?" for each mom and bring a large mirror. Choose a verse from week 8. Write it on a card or dry-erase board. Don't forget the index cards and markers.

Activity: Set the mirror up where all the moms can see it. Sit in a circle. Ask the ladies, "When you look in a mirror, who do you see?" When others look at us, it would be great for them to see Jesus. Play "Mirror of Your Heart" (track 1 on the *Hold You, Mommy* CD).

Questions:
1. How do you reflect Jesus to your kids?
2. What have you said about yourself as you were getting dressed or looking in the mirror that can influence your children's view of themselves?
3. Can you remember a time that you 'fessed up for a mess up? How did it make your heart feel? Were there still consequences that followed?

Closing: When you give the ladies their copy of "Who Am I?" (Appendix 3), talk about who we are in Christ.

Week 8: Learning to Lean

Preparation: Pre-make a phone list with the names and numbers of each lady in your group. Make enough copies to give one to each mom. Choose a verse from week 9. Have markers and index cards available.

Activity: Distribute a copy of the phone chain to each mom in your group. Explain that once you start the phone chain, they will be responsible to call the next name after theirs on the list. When someone calls them, they are to share with the caller their biggest struggle for the day. The last person on the list should call you, the leader.

Questions:
1. Why is it important to have friends with whom you can share?
2. When do you struggle with loneliness?
3. Moms with children older than yours can sometimes give insight into what's ahead. What questions would you ask them if you had the opportunity to have lunch with them?
4. What did God teach you this week?

Week 9: Mouth Monitor Needed

Preparation: Pick a verse from week 10; collect index cards and markers.

Activity: Play "Gossip" in a circle. One person thinks of some silly sentence and whispers it to the next person. The last person has to say aloud what they think the first person said. No repeating!

Questions:
1. Give an example of ways you've seen your words build up or tear down your children or husband.
2. Do you suffer from STMI—otherwise known as gossip? How have you been affected by gossip?
3. How do you introduce your children to others?

Week 10: The Honorable Role of Serving

Preparation: Bring praise and worship music, small flat tubs (from the dollar store), rags, towels, sweet smelling soap, and maybe lotion. Have a verse ready from week 11, and don't forget the index cards and markers.

Activity: Read aloud John 13:1–17, the passage that describes Jesus washing the feet of His disciples, a task normally performed by a servant. As the leader, turn the lights down low, put praise and worship music on, and wash the feet of the ladies. (If there are several ladies in your group, you might want to recruit some help.)

Questions:
1. How do you relate to the big-mouth mama?
2. Describe how the changes in your life have moved you from selfish to selfless.
3. How would you describe your attitude when you serve your family?
4. How will your attitude be changed when you realize that serving your family is serving Jesus?

Week 11: Growing Trust

Preparation: Bring several blindfolds. Pick a verse from week 12, and don't forget the index cards and markers.

Activity: Pair the moms up and have them take turns leading each other (while one is blindfolded) through a tight space. Discuss how it felt to have to depend on someone else when you couldn't see where you were going.

Questions:
1. What is your greatest fear?
2. What burdens are you bearing alone that you need to entrust to God? Have you done that today?
3. Do you know someone who is grieving? Or are you going through grieving?
4. Is there something, large or small, that is clouding your life, making your days dark?

Week 12: Hanging On to Hope

Preparation: *Hold You, Mommy* CD and CD player. Optional: If there has been a recurring theme in your time together, find a symbol that portrays that theme that you can give to each lady as a reminder that God is our hope.

Activity: Have each woman share what the study has meant to her over the past twelve weeks, and present your reminder, if you were able to find one. (Please don't stress about it if you can't find one.)

Questions:
1. What do you look forward to when you think about heaven?
2. Can you find comfort in knowing that Christ will never change? How does that fact apply to the changes you are going through now?
3. Has God been nudging you to do something that doesn't make much sense? What "step" of obedience do you need to take?
4. Are you willing to allow God to change your dreams to accomplish His plans through you?

Closing: Play "Hold You, Mommy" (track 7) from the CD.

Remembertations

AT AGE FOUR, Avery and Crislynn, our youngest daughters, were busy planning a party. (Life is a party with those two!) They were planning the menu, which of course included lemonade, peanut butter and jelly (high on the list!), and for dessert they picked cake, cookies, and candy. Forget healthy—they were going for fun food!

Deep into the planning, I saw them busily writing something. I asked them what they were doing. "We're making the rememberta-tions," they replied. I smiled at their mix-up: *remembertations* instead of *invitations*. But it makes sense. Sending a rememberta-tion is a great way to remind someone about a party, don't you think?

We would like to offer you a "remembertation" as you go through this study. You are *invited* to *remember* (memorize) these key verses that will carry you through your days as a mom. The words will inspire and encourage you to lean on the Lord during these amazing yet trying days.

Each week your leader will give you a verse to copy onto index cards. Take the card home and put it in a prominent place in your home. Then you can be reminded of God's love for you as you wash dishes, fold laundry, brush your teeth, fix your daughter's hair, wash your son's grubby hands, etc. Or you could put the card by your bed so you'll see it at night and before your feet hit the ground in the morning. Even if you don't memorize it, you'll have God's Word in front of you, and that's always a good thing!

Who Am I (in Christ)?

1. **A new creation** . . ."If anyone is in Christ, he is a new creation; the old has gone, the new has come!" (2 Corinthians 5:17).

2. **An ambassador** . . ."We are therefore Christ's ambassadors [to our families], as though God were making his appeal through us" (2 Corinthians 5:20).

3. **No longer a slave to sin** . . ."For sin shall not be your master, because you are not under law, but under grace" (Romans 6:14).

4. **A temple** . . ."For we are the temple of the living God" (1 Corinthians 6:16).

5. **God's workmanship** . . ."For we are God's workmanship, created in Christ Jesus to do good works, which God prepared in advance for us to do" (Ephesians 2:10).

6. **Loved** . . ."I pray that you . . . may . . . grasp how wide and long and high and deep is the love of Christ, and to know this love that surpasses knowledge" (Ephesians 3:17–19).

7. **On His mind** . . ."When I look at the night sky and see the work of your fingers—the moon and the stars you have set in place—what are mortals that you should think of us, mere humans that you should care for us?" (Psalm 8:3–4 NLT).

8. **His forever** . . ."I am convinced that neither death nor life, neither angels nor demons, neither the present nor the future, nor any powers, neither height nor depth, nor anything else in all creation, will be able to separate us from the love of God that is in Christ Jesus our Lord" (Romans 8:38–39).

9. **Held in his hand** . . ."I give them eternal life, and they shall never perish; no one can snatch them out of my hand" (John 10:28).

10. **Forgiven** . . ."If we confess our sins, he is faithful and just and will forgive us our sins and purify us from all unrighteousness" (1 John 1:9).

11. **His child** . . ."What marvelous love the Father has extended to us! Just look at it—we're called children of God! That's who we really are" (1 John 3:1 THE MESSAGE).

Endnotes

Week 2

1. Elizabeth Borton de Trevino, *I, Juan de Pareja* (New York: Farrar, Straus & Giroux, 1966), 58.
2. Helen Lemme (words and music), "Turn Your Eyes Upon Jesus," Singspiration, Inc., 1922, 1950.
3. Steve Green, *Hide 'em in Your Heart,* Volumes 1, 2, and 3, Sparrow Records, 1992. *Good Seeds,* LLC, (Franklin, TN: Provident Distribution Inc.).

Week 3

1. Charlotte Lynas, *Jonah,* self-published, n.d., 58.
2. Andrew Murray, *Abiding in Christ* (New Kensington, PA: Whitaker House, 1979), 145.
3. John Sherrill, "Pencil in Hand —a surprising (and surprisingly effective) way to pray," *Guideposts,* March 2005, 76–80.

Week 4

1. Sarah, Stephen, and Grace Mally, *Making Brothers and Sisters Best Friends* (Cedar Rapids, IA: Winters Publishing, 2002), 20.

Week 5

1. Adapted from an idea in *10-minute Life Lessons for Kids* by Jamie Miller (New York: HarperCollins Publishers, 1998), 27–29.

Week 8

1. Taprina K. Milburn, "Innocent Gossip?" *Focus on the Family* magazine, February, 2000.

Week 9

1. Fred Hartley Jr., *Parenting at Its Best,* (Grand Rapids, MI: Baker Book House, 2003); found on *Christian Parenting Today* online, Summer 2004, Vol. 16, no. 4, 28. *www.christianitytoday.com.*
2. "Bless Your Children, Picturing a Bright Future," *Focus on Your Child, www.family.org* (accessed January 7, 2006).

Week 10

1. Used by permission of Megan Breedlove.

Week 11

1. Steve Green, *Hide 'em in Your Heart,* volume 1, Sparrow Records, 1992.

LAURIE AND SHARON (2MOMS) are wives, moms, speakers, and singers who began a ministry for mothers in 1999. With their husbands, Charles and Pat, and children (seven in all) accompanying them, these sisters have shared inspiring stories and songs with women in 40 states and other parts of the world. Bringing a very *real* message of hope in Christ, Laurie and Sharon encourage thousands of moms through their books and music, the *Mom and Loving It* conferences, and mom-e-moments (free email devotionals).

MOM RESOURCES FROM SHARON AND LAURIE:

Hold You, Mommy —This CD of twelve original songs leads moms to slow down and enjoy the time they have with their children in this season of mothering.

Mom...and Loving It (Bethany House) —Their first book has been a breath of fresh air to many moms, offering hope, laughter, and healing tears as they gently share God's love and design for mothering. With questions at the close of each chapter, the book can be used as a group study.

For more information about hosting or attending a *Mom and Loving It* conference, having Laurie and Sharon speak at your event, ordering resources, or receiving their mom-e-moment via email, visit their Web site: *www.momandlovingit.org*

Sharon and Laurie would love to hear your comments about their books, conferences, music, or emails. You can contact them at mail@momandlovingit.org or

MOM AND LOVING IT, P.O. BOX 286, WHITESBORO, TX 76273
888-95-2MOMS, WWW.MOMANDLOVINGIT.ORG

Can Today's Mom Really Find Contentment in Her Frantic Pace?

If you're feeling discouraged, guilt-ridden, frazzled, or just plain tired, this book about real motherhood will be just what you need to gain new enthusiasm for the job. Combining a frank and sometimes funny style with lots of relevant stories and helpful tips, Sharon and Laurie share how you can find joy even in the most difficult circumstances. If you want to love being a mom, dive right in—this book will change your heart!

finding contentment in REAL life

laurie lovejoy hilliard ❋ sharon lovejoy autry

mom...
and
loving it!

"Practical and refreshing! Every mom will benefit from their helpful advice, powerful wisdom, and heartfelt stories."

—KAROL LADD
Bestselling author of
The Power of a Positive Mom

◈ BETHANYHOUSE